The Village Atlas

The Growth of North
& West Yorkshire
1840-1910

The Village Atlas

The Growth of North
& West Yorkshire
1840-1910

The Alderman Press

Published by The Village Press Limited
7d Keats Parade, Church Street, Edmonton, N9 9DP.

April 1990

British Library Cataloguing in Publication Data

The Village Atlas: the growth of North & West Yorkshire, 1840- 1910.
  1. Yorkshire, 1767-1770. Maps. Facsimiles
  I. Bruff, Barry Robson, 1926-
  911.4281

ISBN 1-85540-025-1

Typesetting by Haworth Associates, Winchmore Hill.
Artwork by Active Arts, Winchmore Hill.
Printed and bound in Great Britain
by The Bath Press, Bath, Avon.

Acknowledgements

The maps in this Atlas are reproduced by kind permission of the British Library.

The publishers would like to thank the staff of the Map Library and Photographic
Department of the British Library for their help during the preparation of this Atlas.

The staff of the Reference Library Enfield Middlesex.

Introduction

The Nineteenth Century was for Yorkshire, as for other industrial centres such as Lancashire and The West Midlands, a period of astonishing growth. New inventions brought people flocking from the countryside to the city to work in new factories. Homes had to be provided for them and manors, farms and market gardens were rapidly built over. Towns like Huddersfield, Bradford, Leeds and Sheffield expanded and their outlying villages and hamlets were swallowed up by the town and in many cases ceased to have any identity of their own.

The population of the West Riding as a whole rose from 564,593 to 2,733,688 during the century. The railways arrived in the 1830's and fifty companies were involved in Yorkshire employing thousands of labourers. The travelling time to London was cut to a day and to Manchester to two-and-three-quarter hours. As the stations were built, so suburbs and industrial sites grew around them as manufacturers moved in to cut their transport costs. The canals which had preceded the railways as the major mode of goods transport fell into comparative disuse although some, the Aire and Calder particularly, have continued in use to the present day.

Yorkshire had one advantage over the other industrial centres in that two of its major industries, wool and coal, had been active for centuries. The wool trade and its major centres, Wakefield, Bradford, Leeds, Huddersfield and Halifax, all prospered with the advent of steam driven machinery. Each town tried to outdo its neighbour in the magnificence of its mills and municipal buildings and even its railway stations.

Wool was far from being the only industry in Yorkshire which generated wealth and employment. In the small town of Brighouse, for example, where the population in 1850 was only some 6,000, there were thirteen cotton mills, a large carpet factory, three woollen and worsted mills, eleven wire and card manufacturers, four dyers and nine engineering and iron foundries, as well as confectioners, soap makers, dry salters, glaziers, tanners and brick and tile makers. Cotton spinning was also carried out in a number of the towns in the West Riding. In the middle of the century there were 1,500 workers in the flax mills of Hunslett.

Coal mining was another of Yorkshire's major industries, particularly in the West Riding and the coming of steam increased the demand for workers leading to the use of child labour. To go down the mines at seven years of age was not unknown. It was also an extremely dangerous job in those days. 1,149 miners were killed in pit explosions between 1851 and 1900 and doubtless many more in minor accidents. 361 men died in an explosion at the Oaks Colliery in 1866.

Barnsley. From the middle of the eighteenth century the linen industry thrived in Barnsley and by 1822 there were thirty-two manufacturers in the town. One of them alone, Messrs J J Taylor, employed some 500 people working 259 looms. In the middle of the century the railway line to Hull was built, giving easy access to the coast for Barnsley's developing coal field. The population had risen from only 3,606 in 1801 to 41,086 by 1901.

Bradford. In the last decades of the nineteenth Century Bradford took over from Halifax as the largest worsted manufacturer. A population of 29,704 in 1801 rose to 290,297 by 1901. It was during the years between 1831 and 1861, when the population more than doubled, rising from around 77,000 to 156,000, that the growth was at its most spectacular. Bradford Township itself had increased its population of 6,393 twelve-fold during the century. It must have been like living in a permanent building site.

The manufacturing statistics of the latter end of the nineteenth century make gloomy reading now. New dyes, discovered in England but developed in Germany, brought great prosperity and employment. 1,500 men were involved in the Bowling Dye Works alone, dyeing half a million pieces of cloth a year, each piece approximately sixty yards long. Prior to the invention of synthetic dyes, the cost of the Tyrian Purple to dye a sixty yard piece was £1,000, which explains why purple was a royal colour.

Halifax, a large parish of 82,543 acres made up of sixteen townships, was already a very important town by 1800. Even as early as 1763 it had a population of 41,220 and its wealth was based on corn, wool and cloth. By 1801 its population was 64,434, twice as large as Bradford's and it continued to grow at a rate of some ten to twenty thousand a year until it reached 221,061 in 1901. Yorkshire owes a great deal to its entrepreneurs and innovators and one of these was John Crossley; mills owned by the family gave employment to 4,500 people producing six miles of carpet per day in their Halifax works.

Leeds was the centre of the heavy woollen trade. In 1794 there were 3,240 manufacturers of broadcloth, all of them within a mile or two of the centre of the town, mainly smallholders. The era of steam brought with it the big factories. With the establishment of the Leeds-Liverpool Canal, the Leeds-Hull Canal and the Midland Railway, Leeds had unrivalled connections with both the Atlantic Ocean and North Sea. The population grew accordingly. In the twelve chapelries or townships which made up the city it rose from 53,162 in 1801 to 428,572 by 1901, with increases of 30,000 to 40,000 every decade, the equivalent of one of today's New Towns.

John Barran started his ready-made clothing company in 1855. By 1905 his new factory in Chorley Lane covered two-and-a-half acres and the cutting shed, covering 7,249 square yards, was reckoned to be the largest room in the world. The shoe and leather trade was revolutionised by technical developments during the latter half of the century.

Dewsbury. The centre of the blanket industry was in Dewsbury and the mill of Wormald and Walker was probably the largest in the world. Founded at the beginning of the nineteenth century, by the early 1900's it was using 700 looms, employing 1,500 people and turning out 9,000 pairs of blankets a week.

The railways came in the 1840's, connecting Dewsbury to Huddersfield, Wakefield and Leeds. During this time the population was swelled by the hundreds of men engaged on building them. Dewsbury's population grew from 10,124 in 1801 to 52,400 by 1901.

Huddersfield had a reputation for the finest worsted in the world and its importance is shown by the Factory Returns in 1901. 54,066 were employed in the wool, worsted and shoddy trade. Among the great mill owners were the Crowther family, who built mills along the Colne valley at Marsden, Slaithwaite and Milnsbridge and which essentially became factory villages. There were other villages at Golcar and Longwood. Mr Crowther was a model employer for the time, supplying his workers with breakfast and dinner at a cost of $4^{1}/_{2}$d (2p). Many of the workers must have come from outlying districts because the total population of Huddersfield in 1901 only amounted to 71,888, having risen from 14,400 in 1801.

Wakefield had a cloth hall as early as 1710, much to the disgust of the merchants of Leeds, who immediately set about building one of their own. The town always had a large market and still has for that matter. The corn market was also very important. Wakefield's reputation as a cloth town goes back long before the sixteenth century. The population grew steadily during the nineteenth century at a rate of two to three thousand every ten years. There were larger rises during the latter half, nearly 8,000 between 1861 and 1871 for example. The greater increases during these years occurred in other towns besides Wakefield and have been attributed to better public amenities bringing a spectacular decrease in infant mortality. By 1901 Wakefield's population was 61,938, having risen from 16,597 in 1801.

Sheffield. Sheffield's population increased more than sevenfold during the nineteenth century, from 41,725 to 307,705. A rise of 36,000 between 1861 and 1871 coincided with the growth of the steel industry. The cutlery trade had a crucial monopoly with its hundreds of small workshops in and around the city. The main line railway arrived late in Sheffield because of the difficulty of access due to the city's comparative isolation in the hills. Sheffield's first line in 1838 connected it with Rotherham but it did not connect with Manchester until the late 1840's.

One of the features to be noted in the atlas are the reservoirs. These were constructed during the century as the need for water increased, to supply the ever-growing population and the greater demands of industry. Huddersfield alone built four, during the years from 1827 to 1838, at Langwood, Wessenden and Deanhead. Sheffield built thirteen on the tributaries of the Don and altogether there are now nearly seventy in the West Riding.

Great quantities of water were required to keep canal levels topped up because of the vast volume which was released from the many locks needed to carry the canals over the Pennines. Some idea of the huge requirements of the textile industry at the time can be realised from the fact that the Bowling Dye Works in Bradford alone needed seven million gallons of water per week.

Rotherham, like its neighbour Sheffield, was a steel, coal and iron town. Growth was fairly steady for the first half of the century, the population roughly doubling between 1801 and 1851 to 7,853. It had doubled again by 1871 and almost doubled once more by 1901 to 30,960.

York, an important coaching town in the days before steam, became a major centre for the building and repair of engines and rolling stock with the coming of the railways. The first works were opened in 1848 and by the end of the century 5,500 workers were employed throughout the industry, excluding foot-plate men and it had become York's biggest employer. The effect the railways had on the country generally can be demonstrated by the figures for York. Prior to 1850 the stage coaches had carried around 24,000 passengers from London to York annually but after 1850 the trains were carrying about 340,000 people over the same route. York became a centre for tourists as it was the terminal for both North and South bound traffic and this resulted in the publication of a great number of guide books for the area in the 1850's.

The confectionery trade was employing more and more people as the century wore on. By 1901 over 2,000 people were employed making jam, preserves, sweets, chocolate and cocoa. York's population was also swollen by a large number of Irish immigrants who had presumably made it their home because of railway building. By 1851 over 2,000 were living there. They tended to form close-knit colonies depending on the home county from which they came. Thus the Boynes, Merlerkeys and Colphens from Sligo all occupied one tenement and those from Mayo another.

Doncaster prospered because of its ideal geographical situation on the river Don, initially making it an ideal crossing point for the Great North Road; consequently, later in the nineteenth century it was a natural choice as a railway junction. Eventually, in 1853, The Great Northern Railway built its workshop there.

Since mediaeval times Doncaster has also been the market centre for a rich farming area and one only has to look at the maps to see the convergence of the road, railway and canal networks to sense its importance over the centuries.

Away from the towns the population figures tell a different story because the villages hardly changed at all over the years. Some perhaps doubled their population during the century but others declined as the exodus to the industrial towns began and there were fewer people living in them in 1901 than in 1801. In Whitley near Pontefract the population figure in 1801 was 819; it rose to 1,125 in 1841 but thereafter fell steadily until in 1901 it was only 790. Farnley Tyas near Huddersfield, where 730 people lived in 1801, gradually diminished to 484 inhabitants by 1901, although it had risen to 900 in 1821.

Some of Yorkshire's towns, on the other hand, were built from scratch by the great industrialists, Saltaire by Titus Salt in 1858, Ripley mill for the Ripley Dye Works and Lilycroft for Lister at Manningham.

Queensbury, lying high on the road from Leeds to Rochdale, is the home of the Black Dyke Mills, more famous outside Yorkshire for its brass band than for the cloth it produced. The growth of Queensbury from a tiny village with outlying cottages where weavers practised their trade to a thriving centre was due to John Foster, who in 1822 started his worsted business. By the 1840's there were over 3,000 spindles in operation at the Black Dyke works.

Bringing the railway to Queensbury was a difficult task, involving building the longest tunnel on the Great Northern Line and four streets of houses had to be built to accommodate the navvies.

Copley was another model village built around the middle of the century by Ackroyds near their Copley Mill. A church and library were built on the site, as was a recreation ground and allotments for the workers.

The development of the wool trade, even from its humble beginnings as a cottage industry in the remote valleys, meant that wool had to be transported to and fro for the various stages of manufacture and thus over the centuries a network of pack-horse roads emerged. Many of these tracks form the basis of present day roads and this explains why some of the latter have an almost precipitous descent into the valleys. For convenience, the cottages gradually moved to a central village, albeit still high in the Dales. With the coming of steam and as factories grew in the lowlands, the water mills of the Dales fell into disuse, the remains of some still standing today.

Those villages such as Almondbury, lying on the outskirts of major conurbations, eventually became absorbed into the expanding towns. In contrast, Holme, described as a thriving community in the mid-nineteenth century, declined towards the end of the century as its population migrated down into the valley to Holmfirth (the setting for Last of the Summer Wine), or even beyond to Huddersfield. By the end of the century the population had slipped back to 537, only 235 more than it had been in 1801; its inn, The Fleece, is now the only remaining connection with its past famous trade. There were many other villages or townships in the Dales where the population remained much the same throughout the century, Thurstonland, Chapel Haddlesey, Temple Hirst, Thorpe Wiloughby, Drax, Ledston, Stonebeck and Saxton to name but a few.

The building of turnpike roads directly affected the growth of major towns in the nineteenth century; the Kendal - Keighley - Halifax, Halifax - Leeds, Halifax - Bradford and Halifax - Rochdale turnpikes were all built in the 1730's and 40's. These in turn linked in with the network of canals, then wharfs; the new steam-powered factories were built alongside them because the canals became the chief carriers of coal, spelling the end of the small, remote, water-powered mills in the hills.

As new roads and canals had engendered growths in towns like Halifax, Bradford,

Leeds and Huddersfield, they automatically became prime sites for railways in the 1830's, adding to the growth of already successful towns rather than stimulating new growth. The first line in Yorkshire was built in 1834 between Leeds and Selby. Leeds - Thirsk brought connections between North and South in 1849. During the 1840's Leeds, Bradford, Skipton, Dewsbury, Huddersfield and Wakefield were all interconnected. Leeds was joined to the Midland link at Normanton and to London via Rotherham. Sheffield's problems have already been mentioned but by 1851 it was connected to both Manchester and Lincoln. In 1874 Leeds was connected via Settle to Carlisle, a line beloved by enthusiasts because of the unrivalled scenery it traverses.

The railways, canals and reservoirs were adding a pleasant dimension to Yorkshire's already spectacular landscape but other industries were changing its face in less attractive ways. Waste from coal mines was dumped as near as possible to the coal face without any thought for the environment and slag heaps proliferated. Only now is some action being taken to remove or soften these blots on the landscape.

The statistics of the time are staggering in today's terms. In the woollen and worsted trade 52,758 people were employed in Bradford, Shipley, Baildon and Clayton; 13,027 in Huddersfield; 12,247 in Halifax and 11,722 in Leeds. The weaving shed at the Shaw Lodge Mills in Halifax, where, amongst other things, the cloth to cover railway seats was made, was 396 yards long and contained 380 looms.

This brief introduction is by no means a complete history of the development of nineteenth century Yorkshire and the maps themselves, for reasons of space, only cover the industrial areas of Yorkshire because that is where the greatest changes took place. The publishers hope that it will be a useful companion-volume to the many books written about Yorkshire, its towns and its cities. The lay-out of the maps is in thirty-two sections, each containing a map from the beginning, middle and end of the century. Just turning the page gives an instant understanding of the great changes that were taking place in the county.

Barry Bruff
London, 1990.

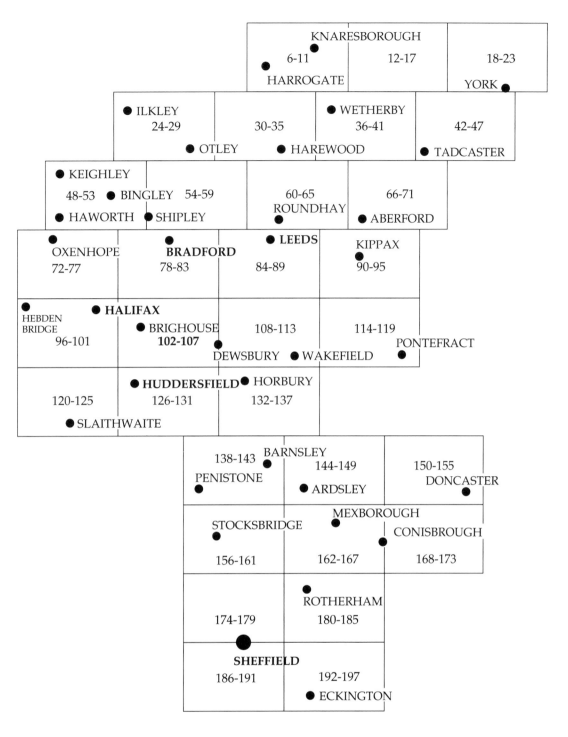

The Maps

Publisher's Note

The maps in this Atlas are based on a scale of two inches to the mile. However, because of the number of different maps involved and the reproduction thereof there may be some minor variations in scale. The age of the maps and the fact that there could be as much as fifteen years difference between the dates of survey of adjoining maps, plus the handling and folding which has taken place over the years, have also meant that there are small differences here and there which are impossible to eradicate.

The publishers have made every effort to minimise these faults and trust the reader will make allowances for any slight imperfections.

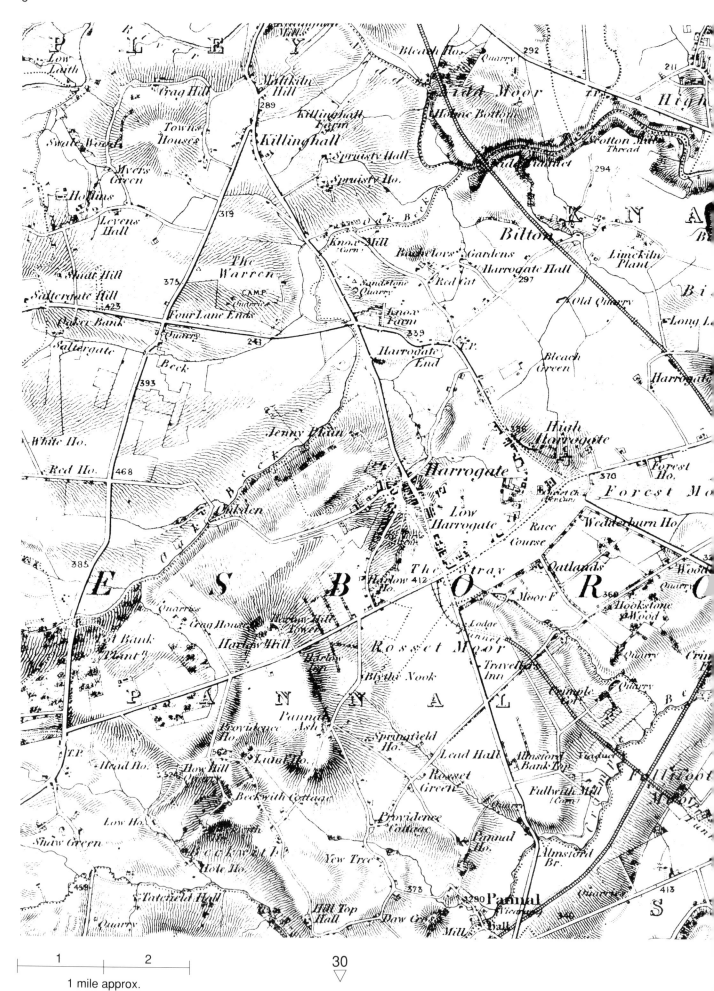

1

2

30

1 mile approx.

Published 1858.

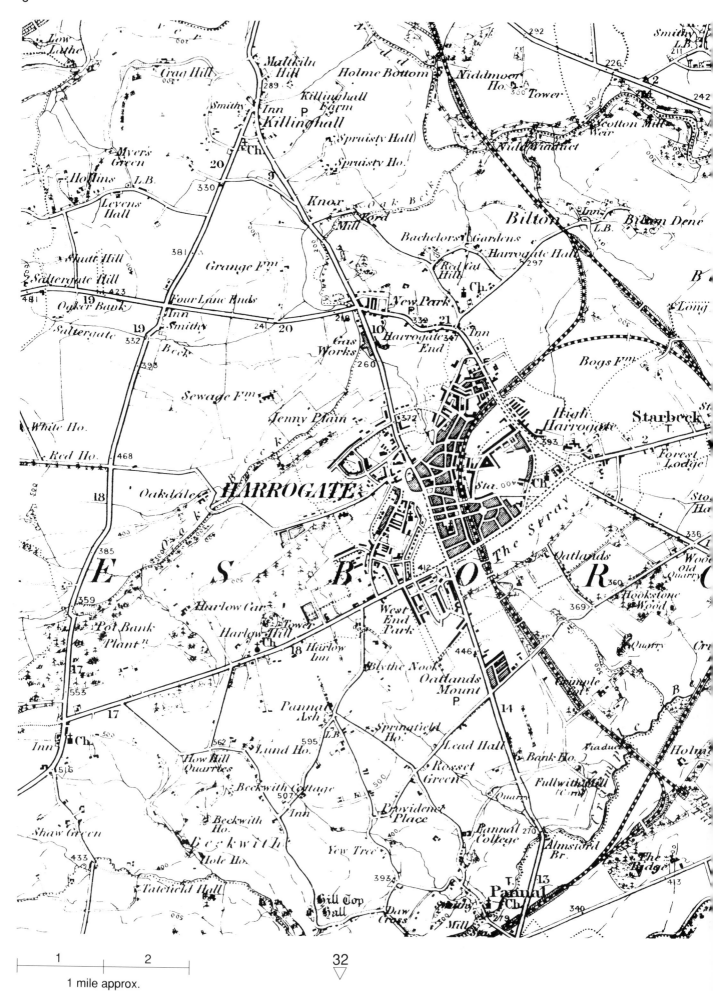

1 mile approx.

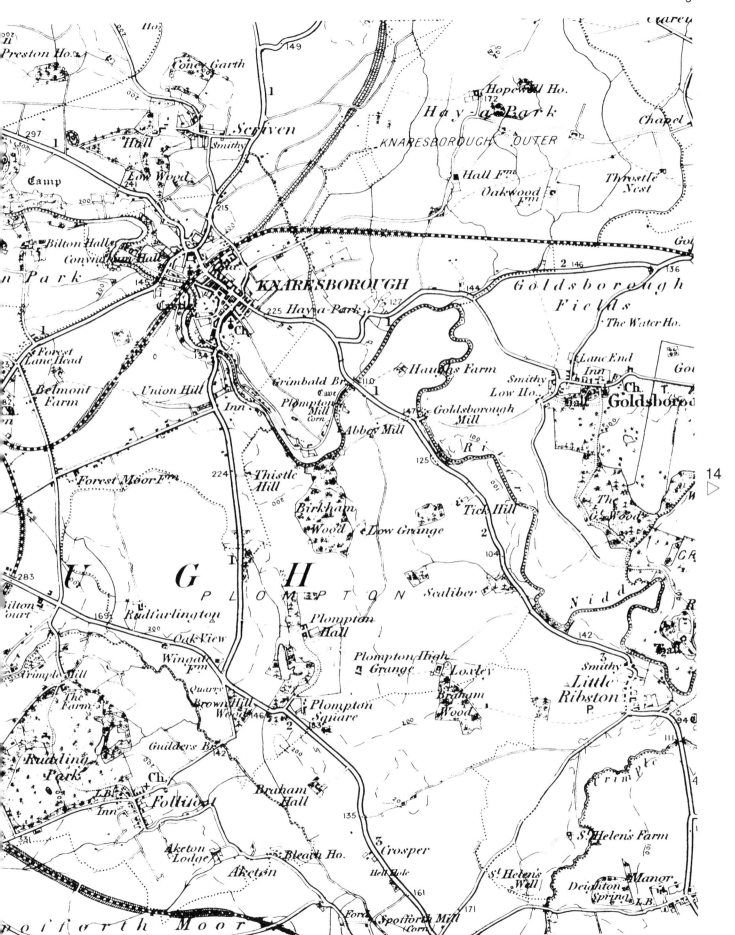

Surveyed 1846 - 52. Revised 1896. Published 1898.

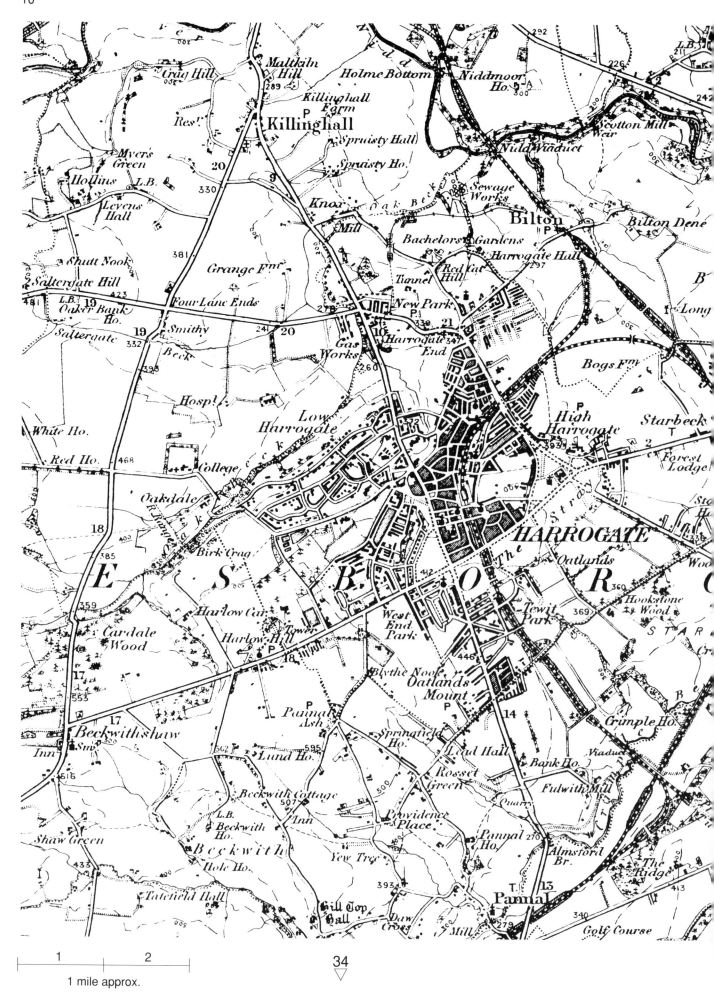

1 mile approx.

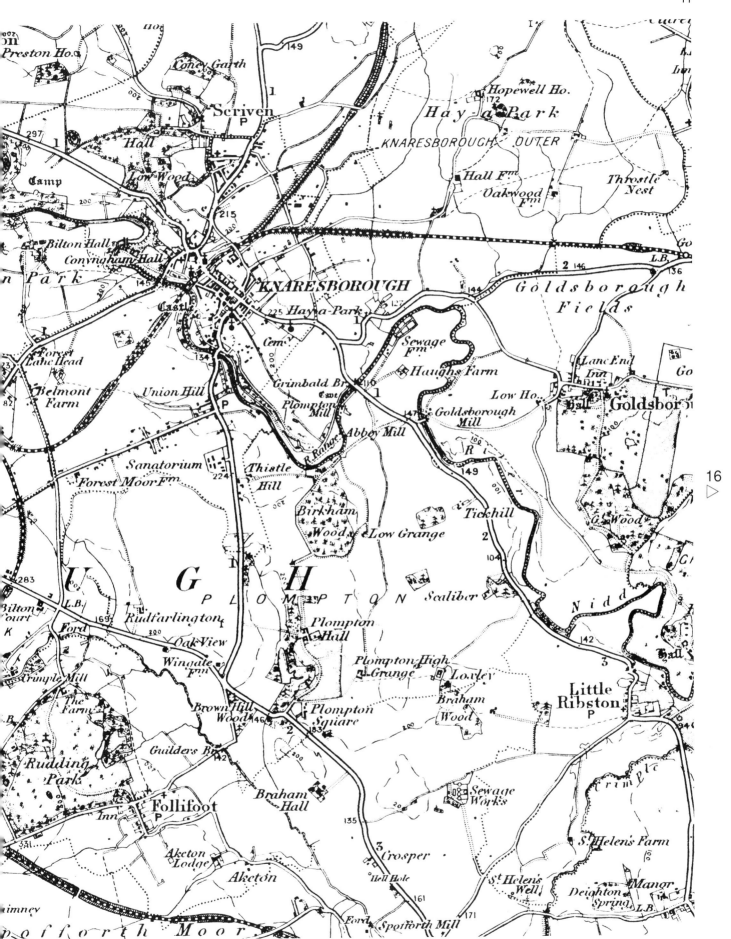

Surveyed 1846 - 52. Revised 1911. Published 1913.

1   2

1 mile approx.

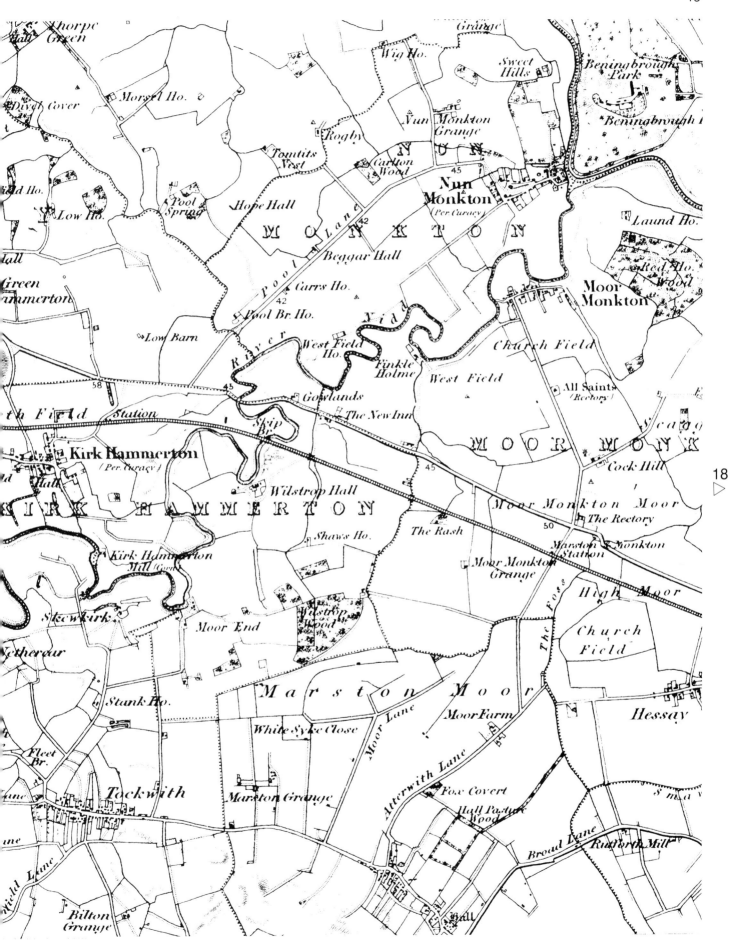

Published 1858.

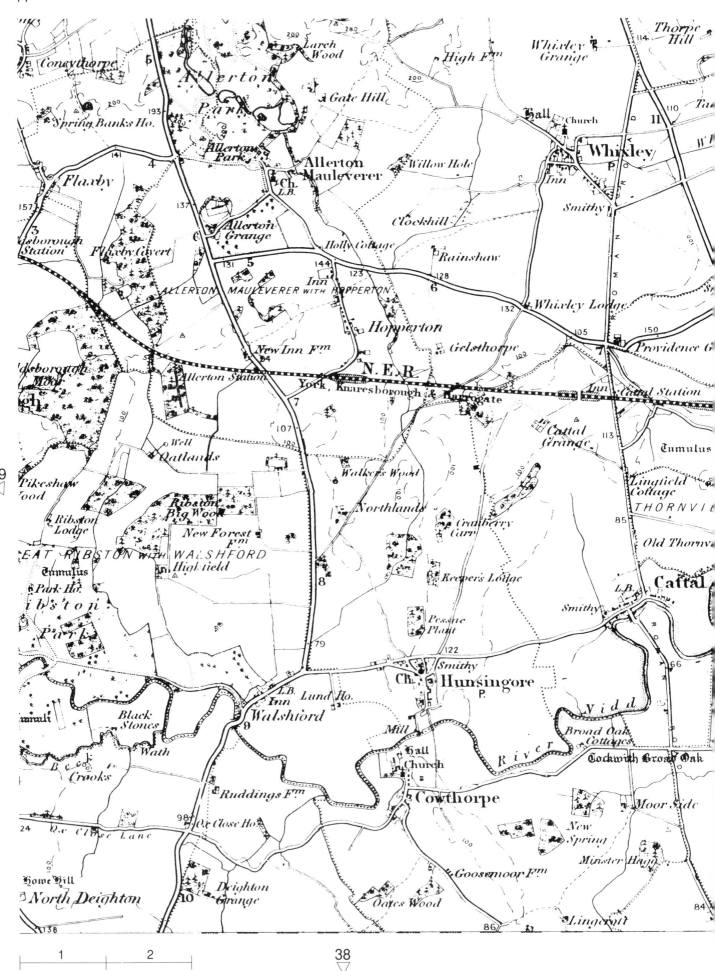

1   2

1 mile approx.

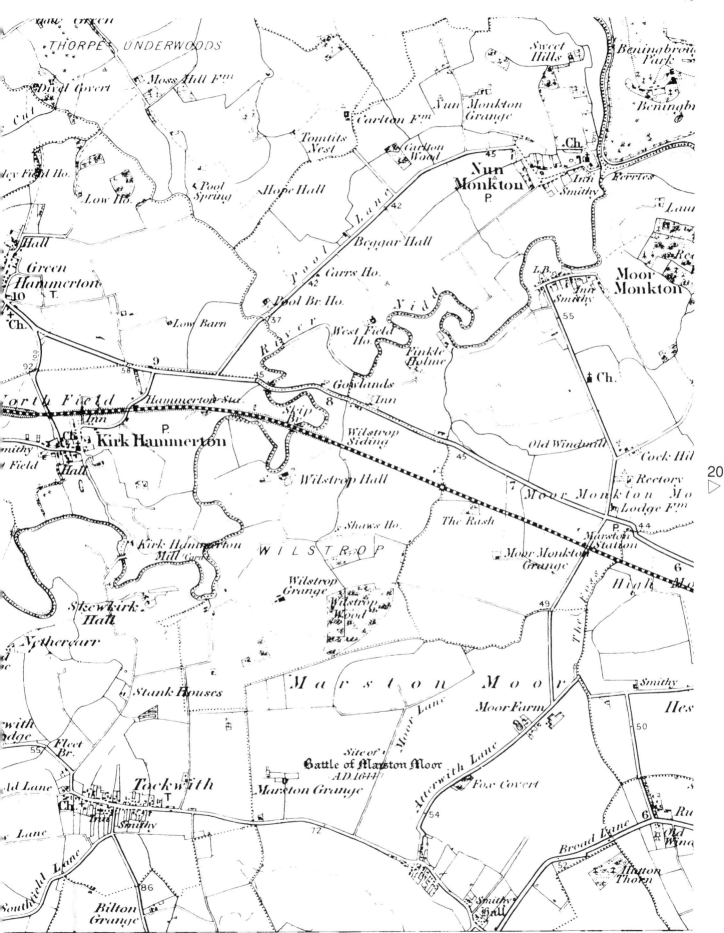

THORPE UNDERWOODS

Moss Hall Fm

Divel Covert

Cut

dey Field Ho.

Low Ho.

Hall

Green Hammerton

10

T.

Ch.

92

58

North Field

Hammerton Sta.

Inn

P.

Kirk Hammerton

Ch.

mithy

Field

Hall

C

Skewkirk Hall

Nethercarr

c

with Lge

dge

55

Fleet Br.

d Lane

Ch.

Inn

Smithy

Lane

86

Bilton Grange

Southfield Lane

Low Barn

Pool Spring

Hope Hall

Pool Br. Ho.

Carlton Fm

Tomtits Nest

Carlton Wood

Beggar Hall

Carrs Ho.

West Field Ho.

River

Nidd

Finkle Holme

Gowlands

Inn

Skip Br.

8

Wilstrop Siding

Wilstrop Hall

Shaws Ho.

WILSTROP

Kirk Hammerton Mill

Cork

Wilstrop Grange

Wilstrop Wood

Stank Houses

MARSTON MOOR

Moor Lane

Battle of Marston Moor
A.D.1644

Marston Grange

Atterwith Lane

Fox Covert

54

72

Nun Monkton Grange

Sweet Hills

Beningbrou Park

Beningb

Ch.

45

Nun Monkton

P.

Inn

Smithy

Ferries

Lau

Re

L.B.

Inn

Smithy

Moor Monkton

55

Ch.

Old Windmill

45

Cock Hil

Rectory

Moor Monkton Mo

Lodge Fm

P.

44

Marston Station

Moor Monkton Grange

High

Mo.

6

The Row

49

Smithy

Moor Farm

Hes

50

Broad Lane

52

Marston Thorn

Smithy

Hall

6

Ru

Old Win

42

42

37

9

45

5

45

7

Surveyed 1846 - 52. Revised 1896. Published 1898.

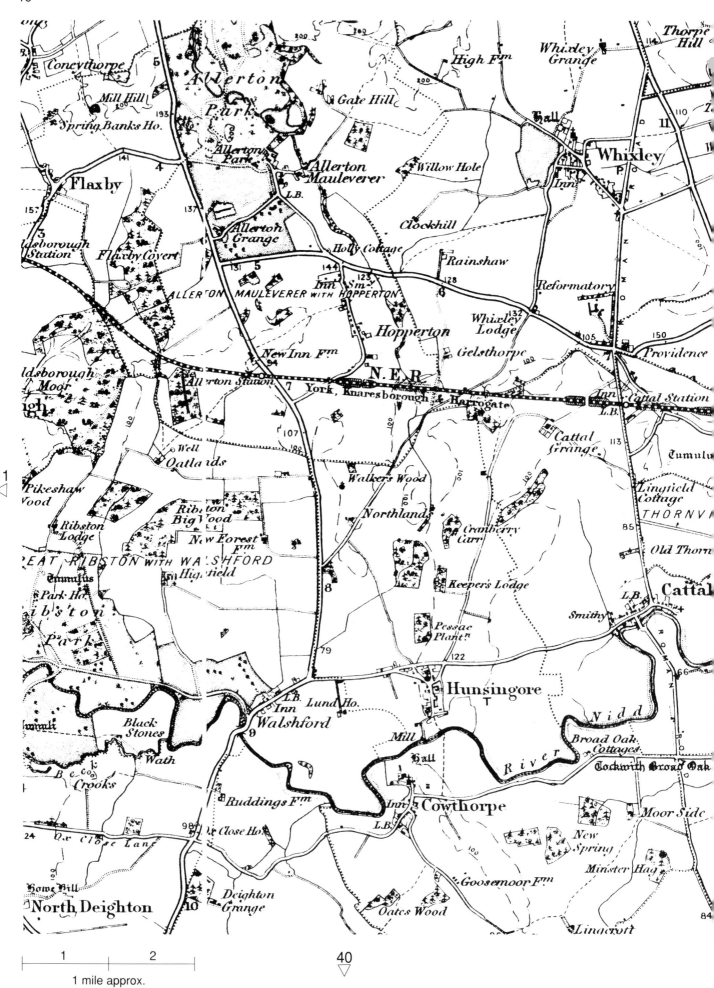

1 mile approx.

40

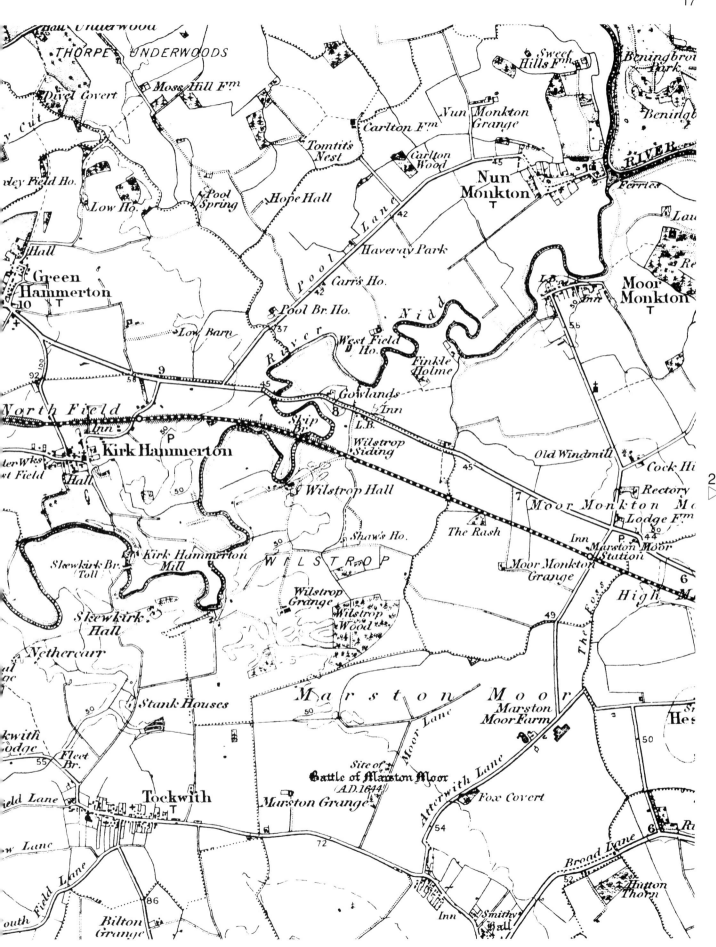

Surveyed 1846 - 52. Revised 1911. Published 1913.

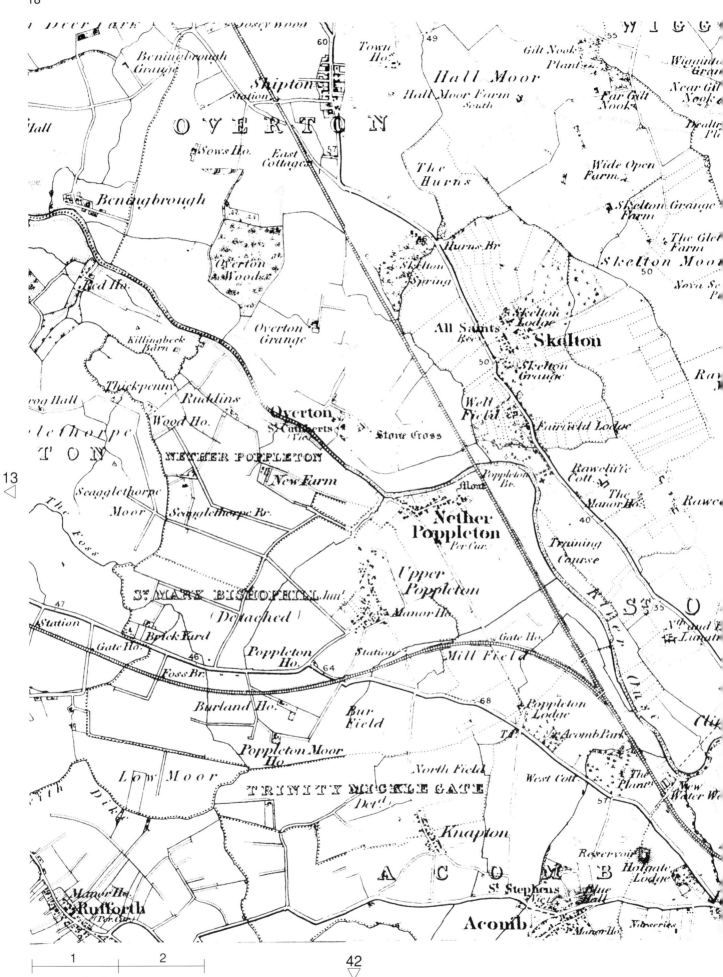

13
◁

42
▽

1   2

1 mile approx.

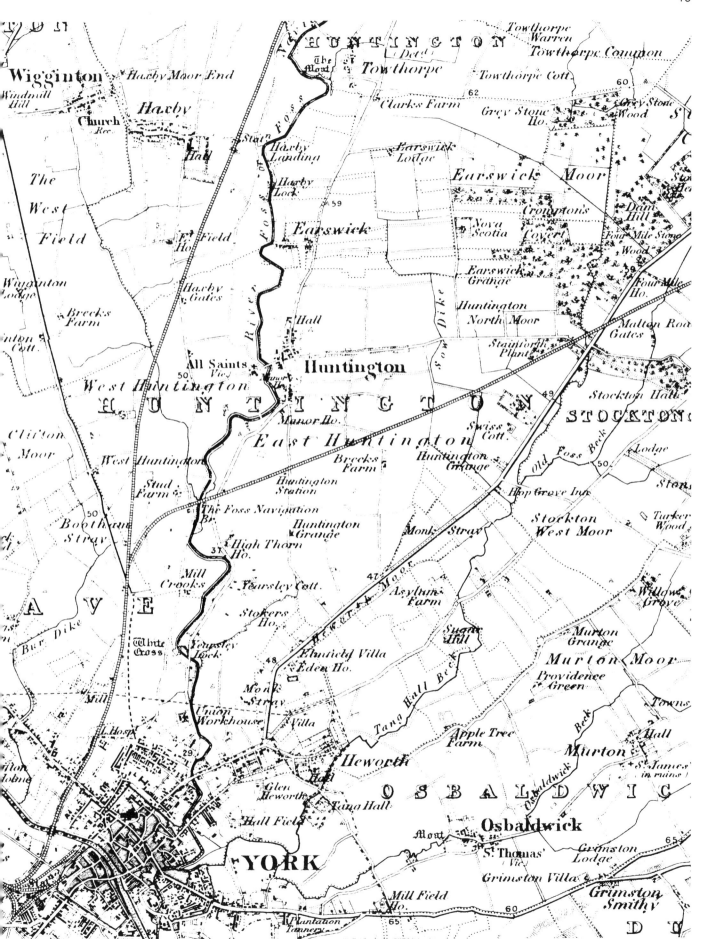

Published 1858.

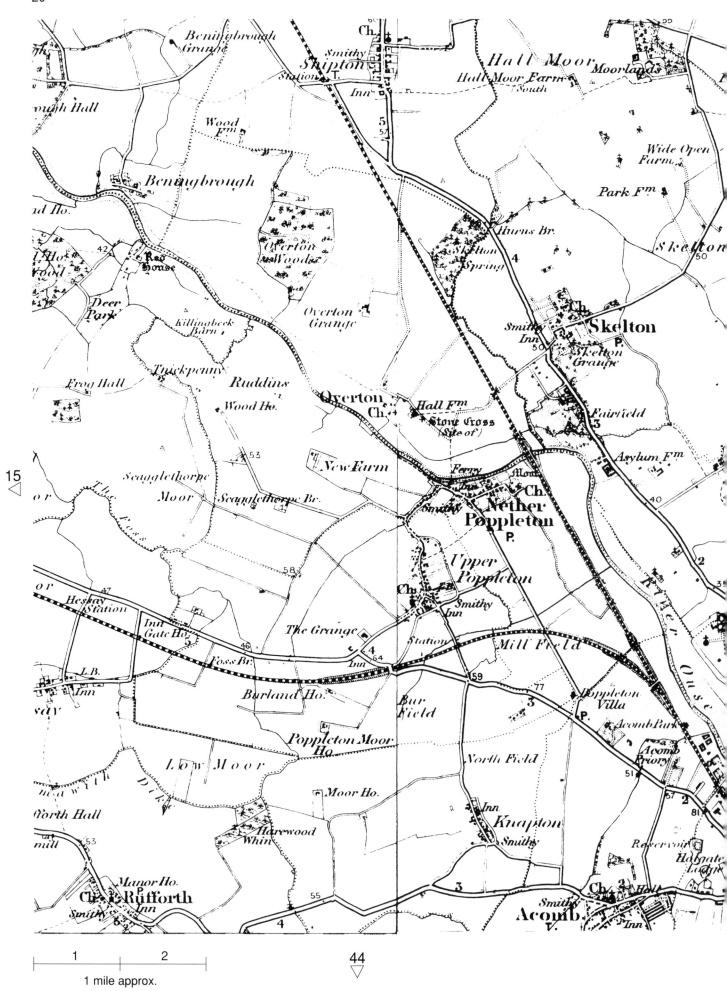

1 mile approx.

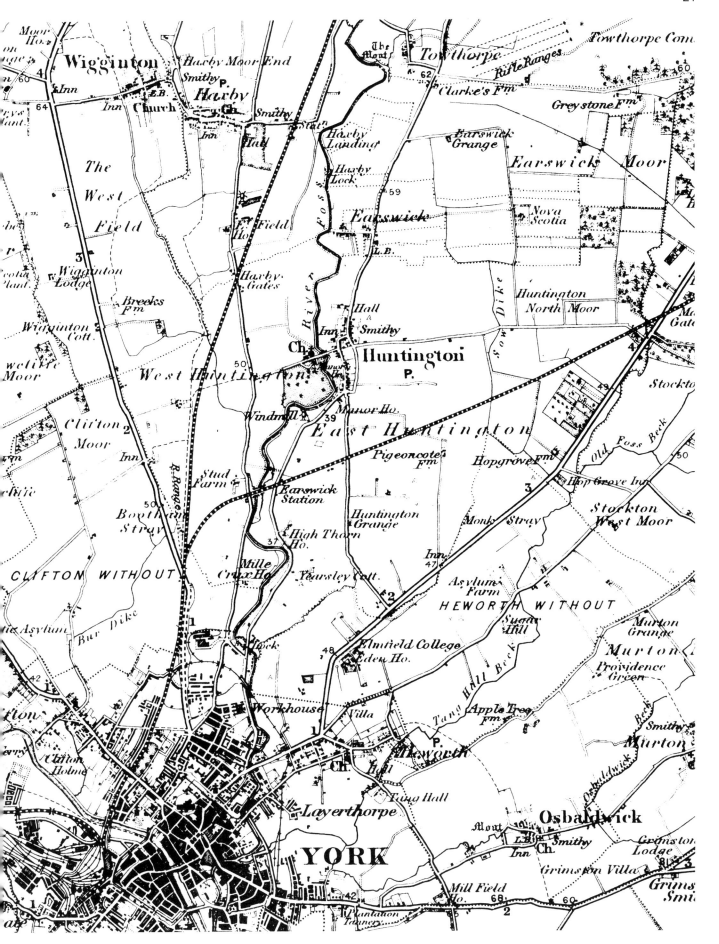

45

Surveyed 1846 - 52. Revised 1896. Published 1898.

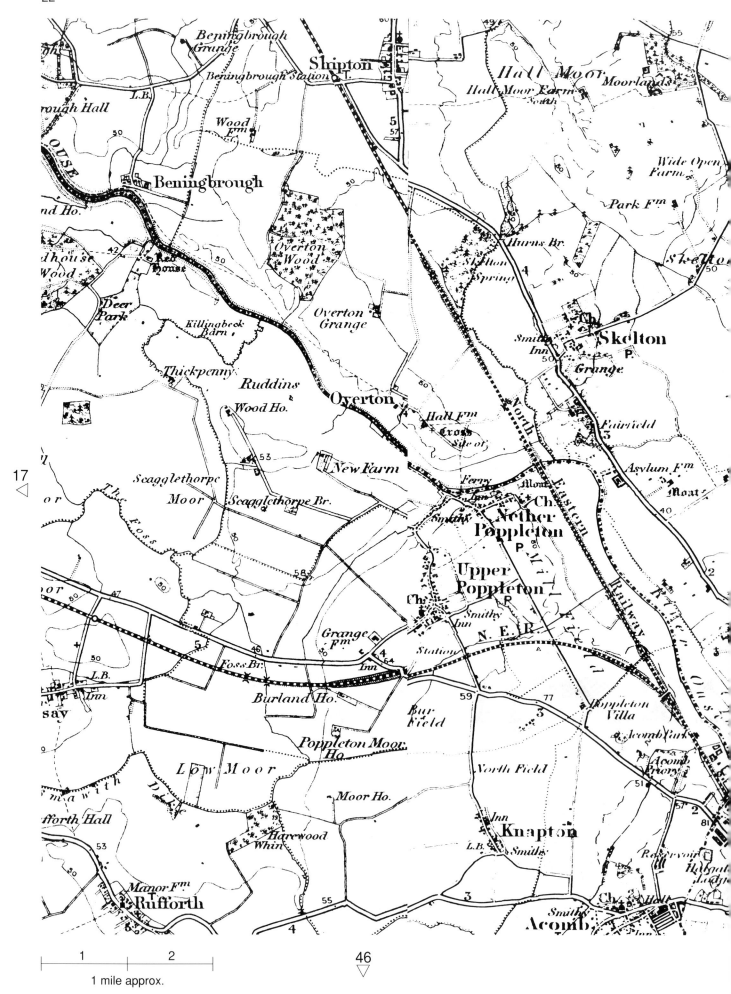

1 mile approx.

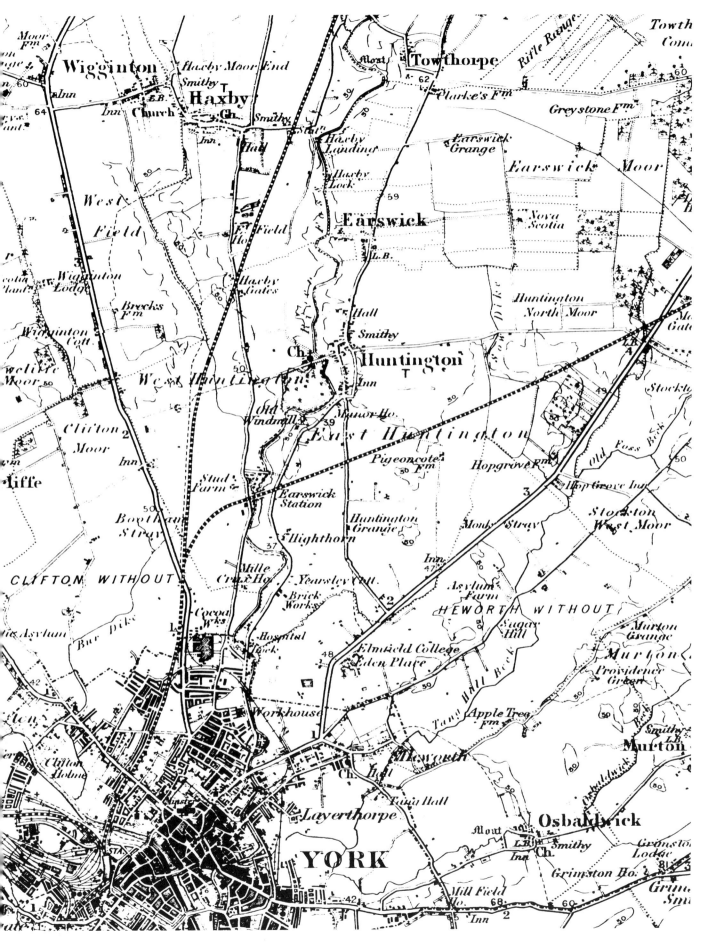

47 Surveyed 1845 - 52. Revised 1904 - 05. Published 1906.

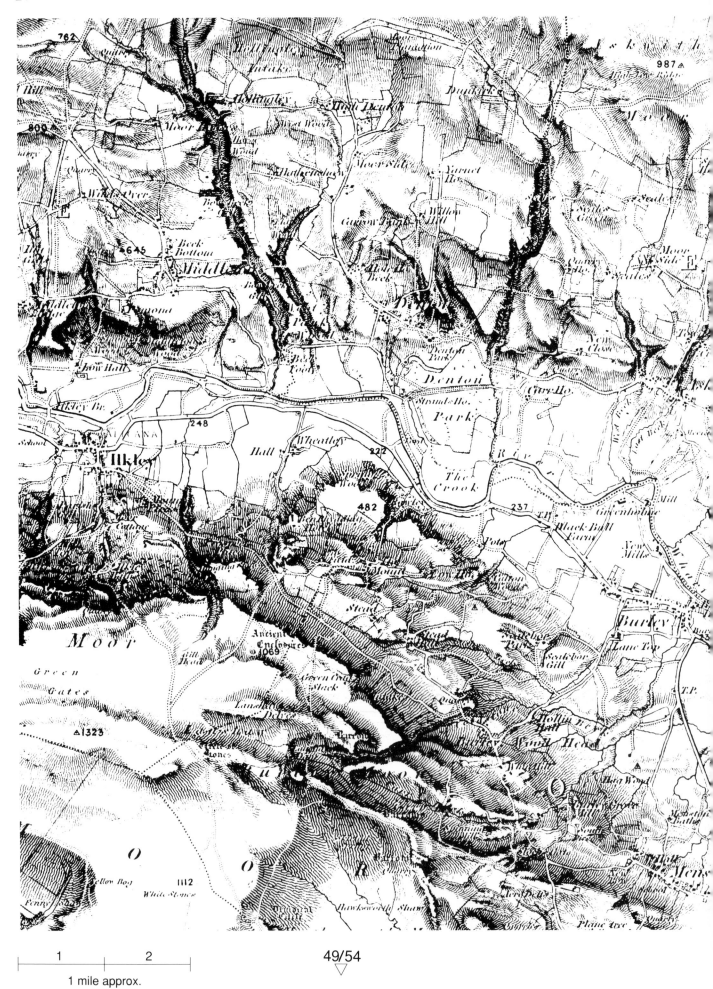

1   2

1 mile approx.

Published 1858.

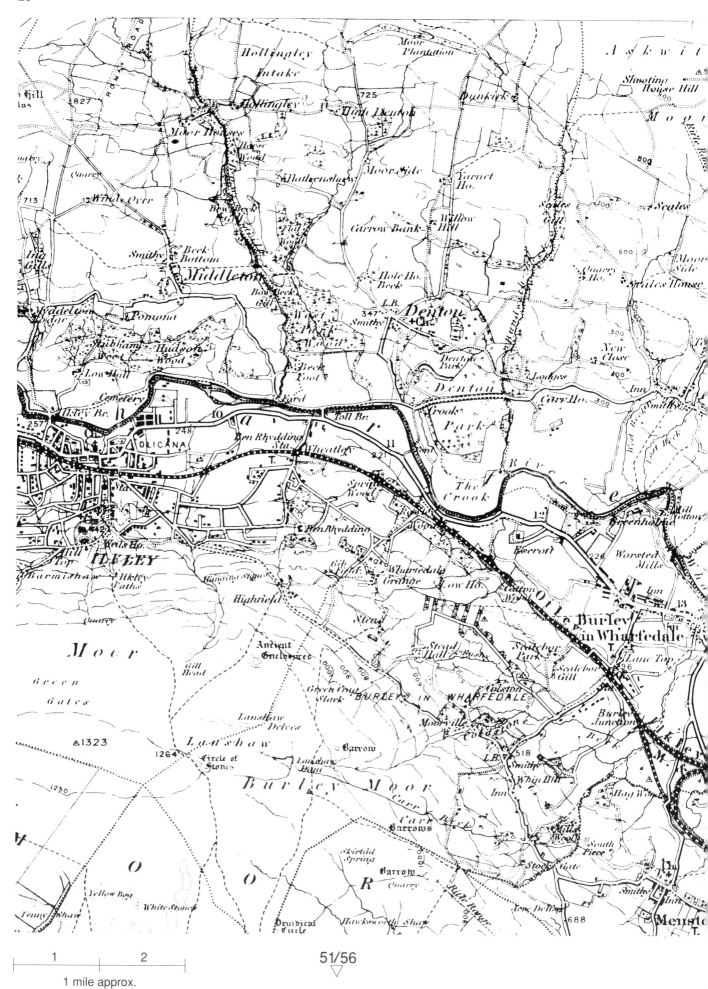

1 2

1 mile approx.

51/56

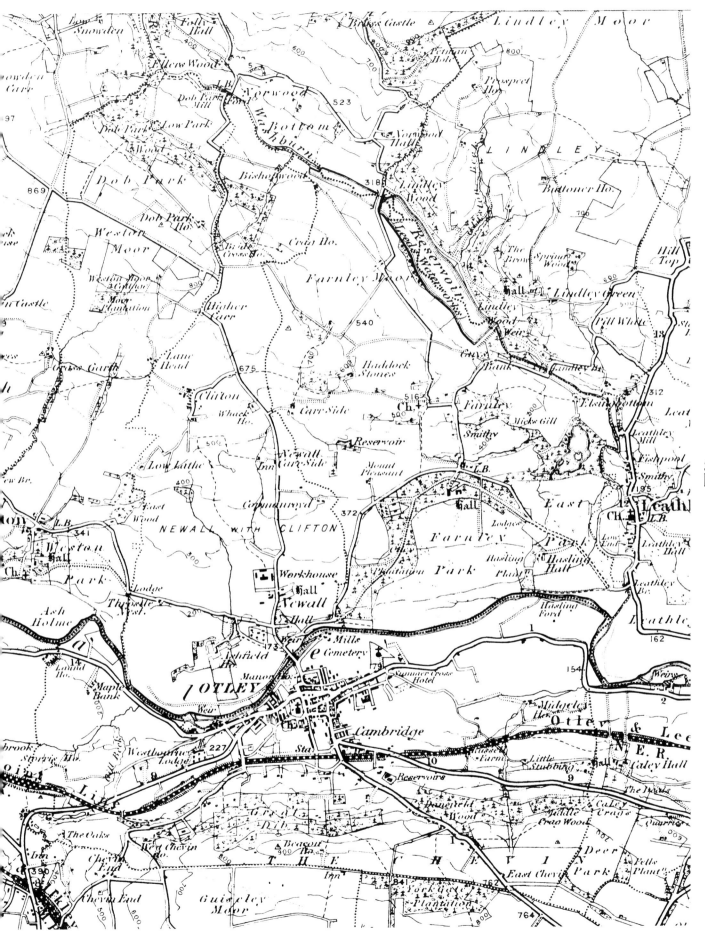

Surveyed 1843 - 49. Revised 1896. Published 1898 - 99.

1 mile approx.

Low Snowden · Folly Hill · Brass Castle · Lindley Moor

Ellens Wood · Fewnall Hole · Prospecthouse Fm

Norwood Bottom · Norwood Hall · LINDLEY

Dob Park · Low Park · Washburn · Bishopwood · 318 · Lindley Wood · Buttoner Ho. · Beckbo

Wood · 869 · Dob Park Ho. · Lindley Reservoir · Leeds Waterworks

Weston Moor · Bridle Cross Ho. · Springs Wood · 700

Weston Moor Cottage · Moor Plantation · 800 · Farnley Moor · Hall · Lindley Green

Higher Carr · 540 · Lindley Wood · Pill White · Weir

Castle · Lane Head · L.B. · 675 · 600 · Haddock Stones · 516 · 600 · Lindley Br. · 312

Grass Garth · Clifton · Carr Side · Farnley · Elsuigbottom Fm · Leathl Mo

NEWALL WITH CLIFTON · 500 · Newall Carr Side · Reservoir · Mick's Gill · Leathley Mill

Low Laith · Inn · Mount Pleasant · Smithy · 400 · Fishpool

Br. · 400 · Copmanroyd Fm · 372 · Hall · East · Leathle · 195

East Wood · 300 · Otley · Farnley Park · Hasling Plant · Hasling Hall · Leathley Hall

Weston Hall · Workhouse · Plantation · Park · Leathley Br.

Park · Ash Holme · Thistle Nest · Hall · Newall · Hasling Ford · 155 · Leathley · 162

Laund Ho. · Ashfield Ho. · Mill · Cemetery · 14

Maple Bank · Manor Ho. · OTLEY · Midgley Ho. · Otle & Leed · N.E.R.

Weir · Cambridge · Russell Farm · Little Stubbing · Caley Fm · The Deals

Storris Ho. · Gill Beck · Westbourne · 227 · Reservoirs · 10 · 9 · Hall · Caley Crags

Line · Great Dib · Danefield Wood · Middle Crag Wood · Caley Crags · Quarrie

Oaks Fm · West Chevin · Beacon Ho. · 900 · THE CHEVIN · Deer Park · Fells Plant

Inn · Chevin End · 390 · Inn · E. Chevin Park · Old

Guiseley Moor · York Gate Plantation · 765

Surveyed 1843 - 49. Revised 1910. Published 1913.

Moor
757

727 △
690

Briscoe Rigg

Moor
Side

Bilberry
Crook

Alder Cur
Ho.

422 New
Covert

Well

Sandston
Quarry

326 △

Holm
Bank

Spring
House

Nab Ho.

Leyfield
Ho.

Beck

Rigton Lodge

Low
594

High
Moor

Moor
Side

America

KIRBY OVER

Nor Rigton

Moat

Wesleyan

Keswick

Swinden

Spout
Ho.

Stainburn

Clay Bank
Ho.

Dunkeswick
Lodge

Low
Moor

Hollin
Hill

Wood Gate Mill

Healthwaite Hill

The Banks

Methodist Chapel

Hub

Weeton
Station

Haggas
Hall

Baileys Whins

Nuby

224

Rudding

Beck

Healthwaite
Hill

25
◁

North
Field

Nuby
Lodge

Winters
Wood

Methodist Chapel

Nook

Weeton

Led Field

Rhudd

Weeton Hill

Rougemont

Stubbins
Ho.

Wescoe Hill

Silver Fort

River Wharfe

River

Castley Ford

Castley

Arthington
Pastures

Bank
151

Sand
Bed

130

Poole Br.

Rotherford

Arthington

The Nunnery

Poole

Poole Crook

Arthington Mills

Arthington Hall

Holt
Farm

Plainville

181

Warren

School

48

Park

Kirskill

Arthington

Arthington
Grange

Linfield
Ho.

The Bog
Plant

H

Kirskill
Hall

Bank Foot

Staircase

Quarry

552

Arthington Bank

Bramhope
Hall

Bramhope Mill

Bank Top

Burder Head Fm

Stub

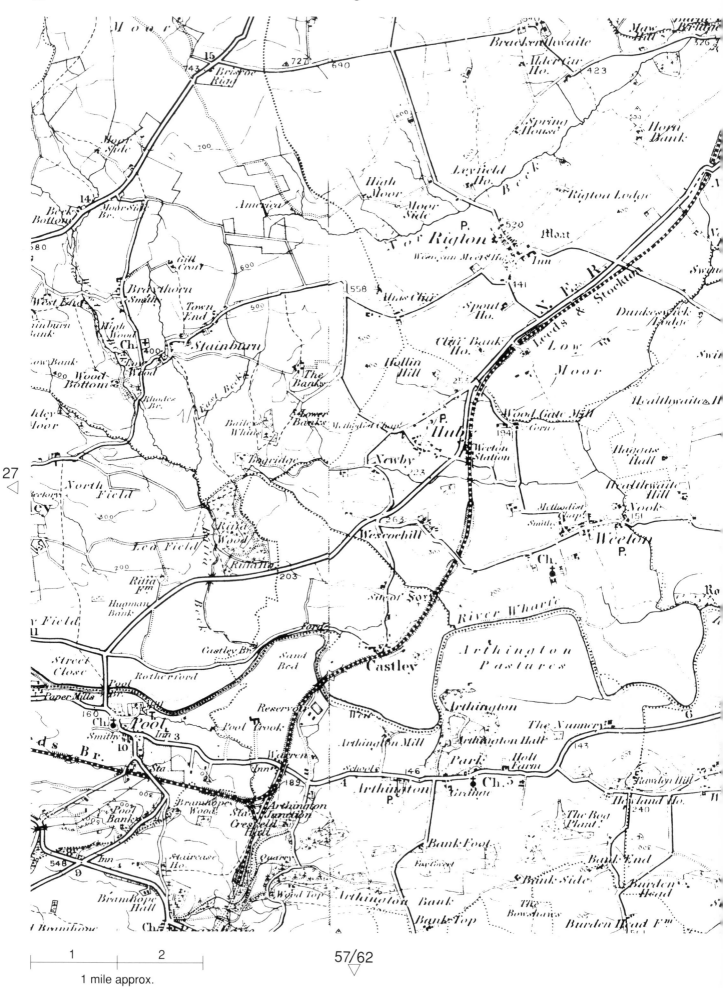

1   2

1 mile approx.

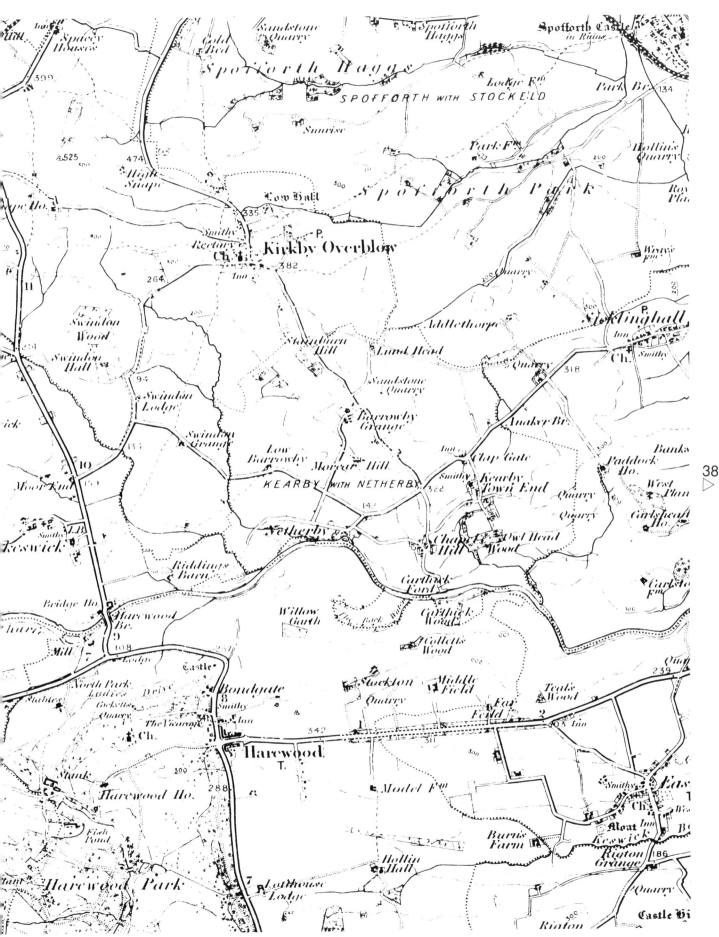

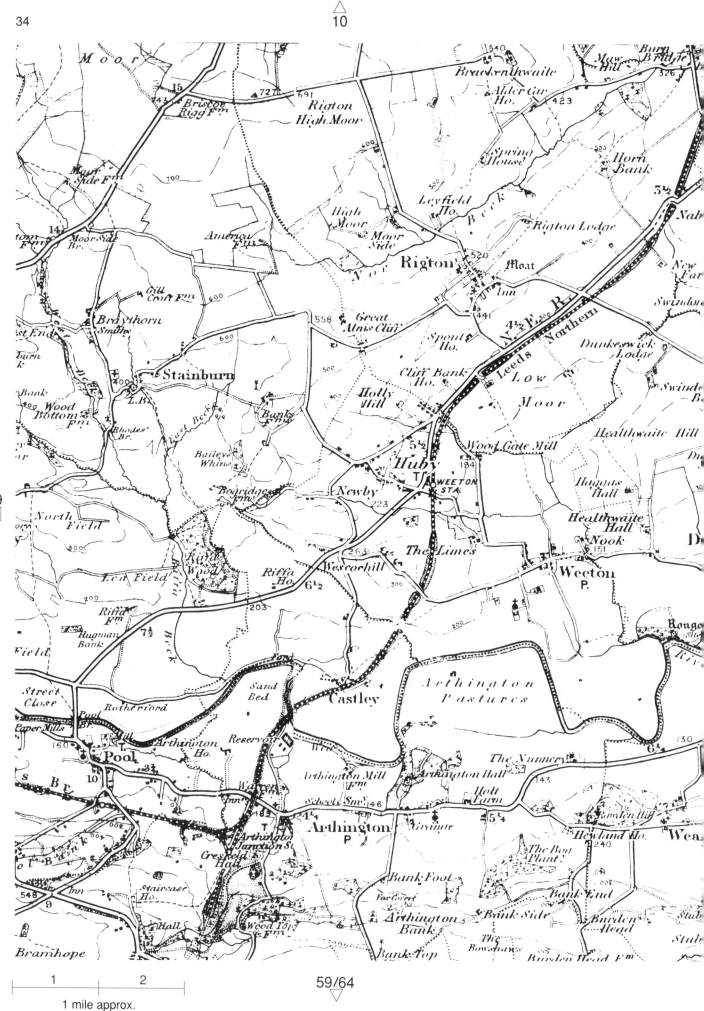

1   2

1 mile approx.

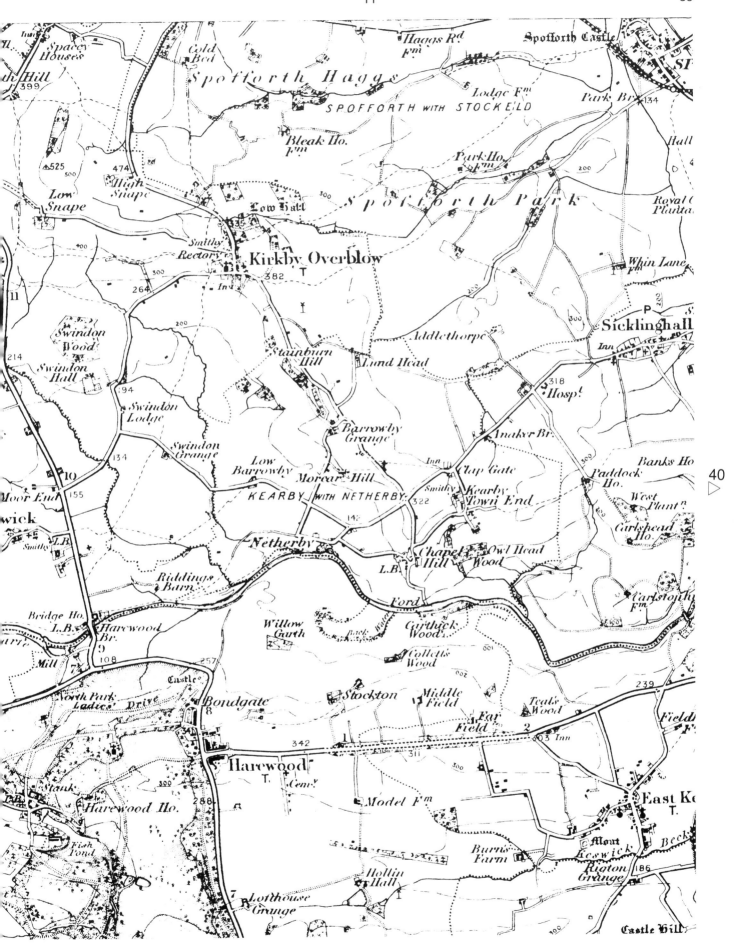

Surveyed 1843 - 49. Revised 1910. Published 1913.

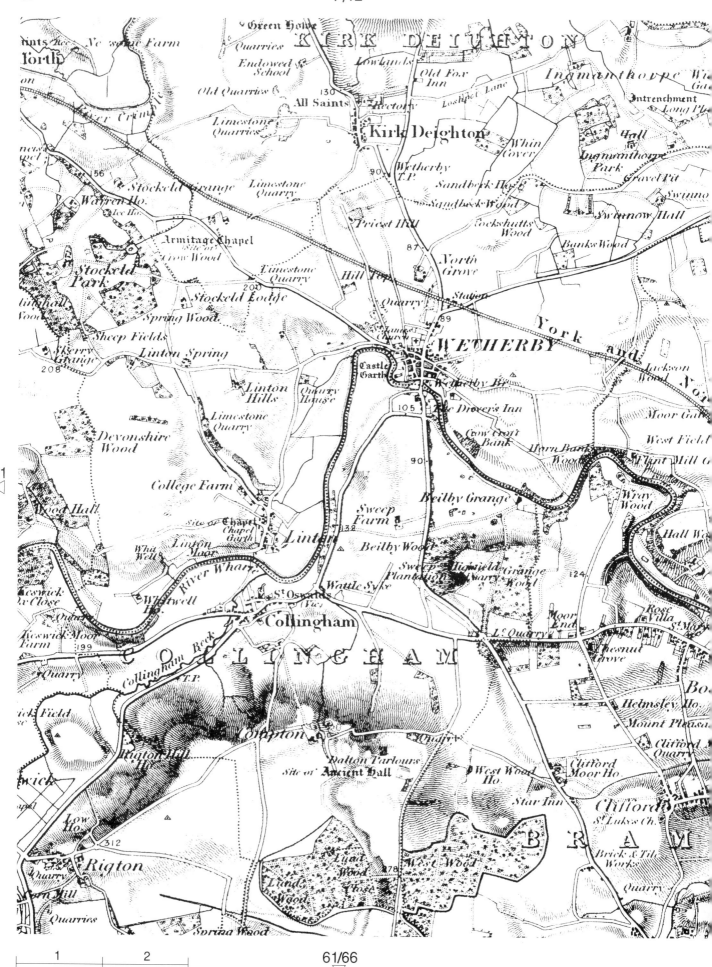

1

2

1 mile approx.

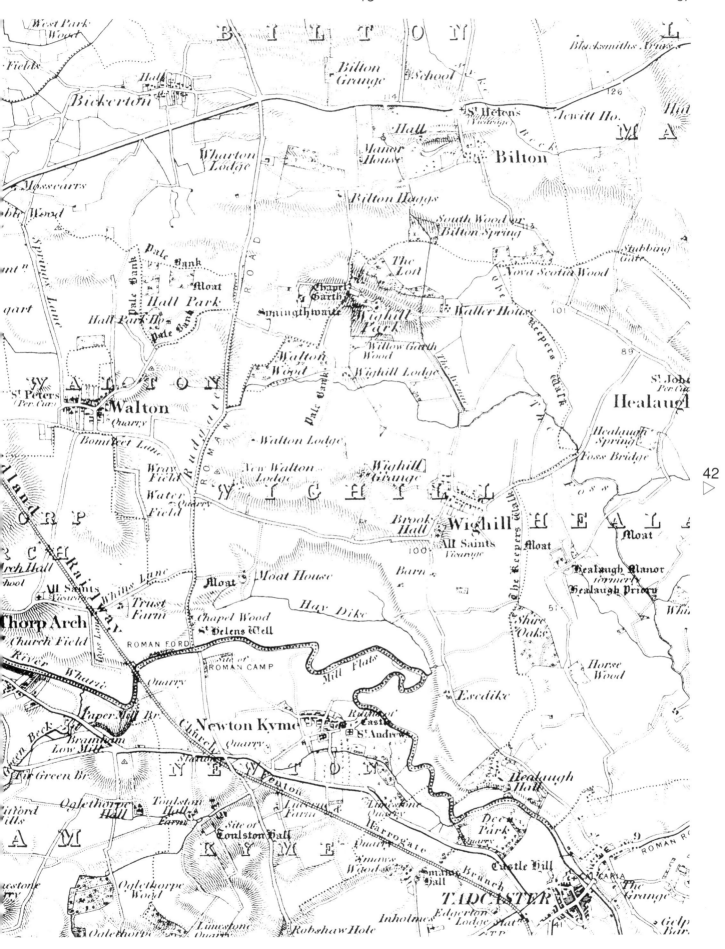

Published 1858.

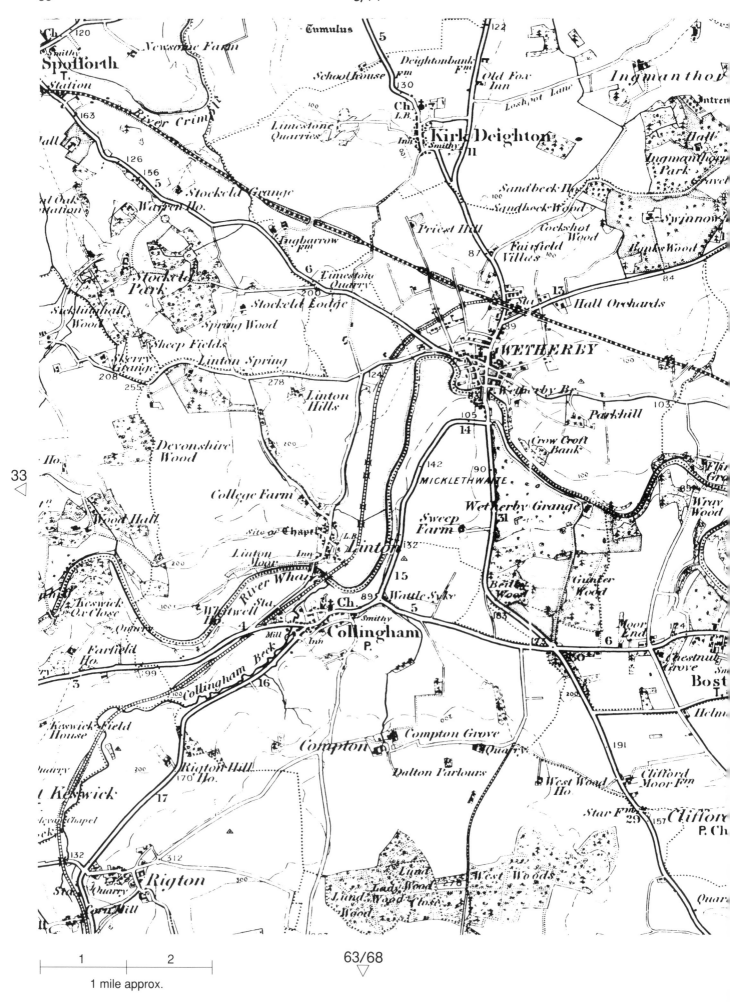

1   2

1 mile approx.

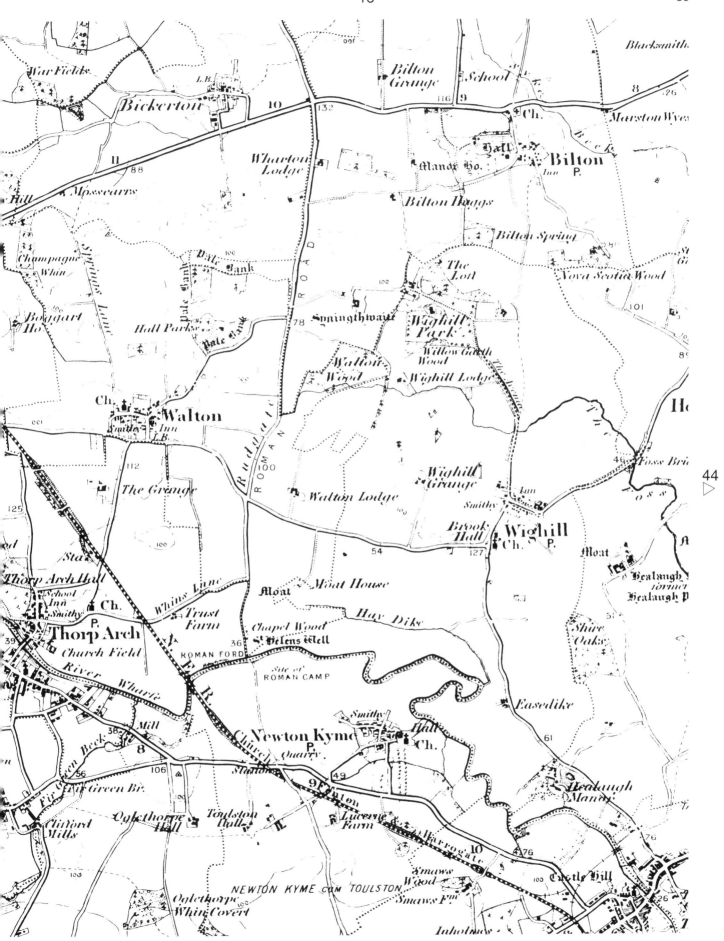

Surveyed 1843 - 49. Revised 1896. Published 1898 - 99.

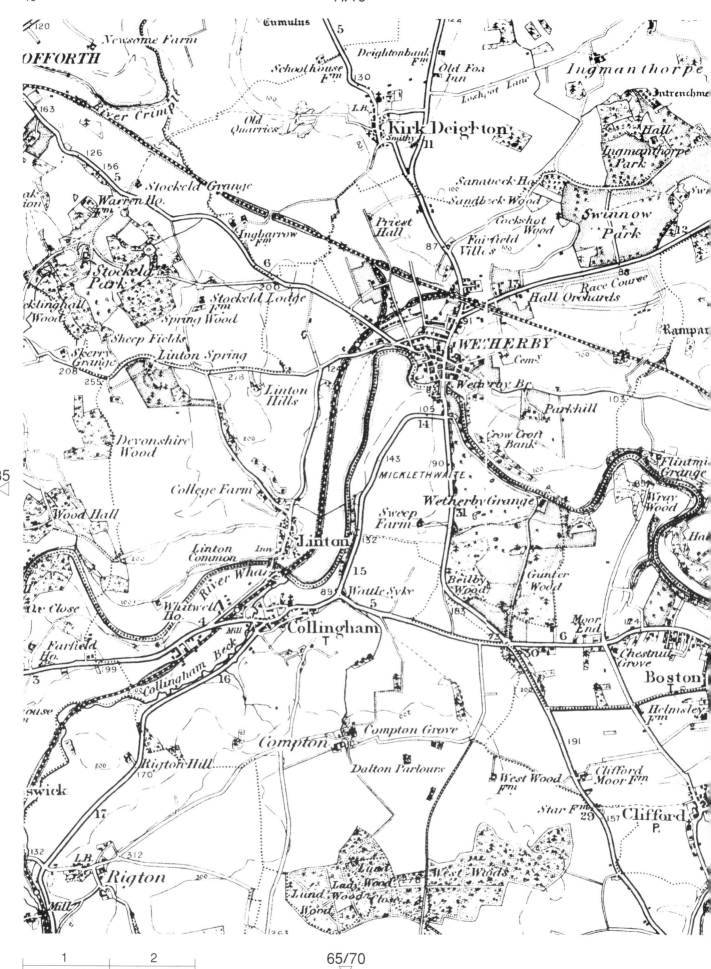

1   2

1 mile approx.

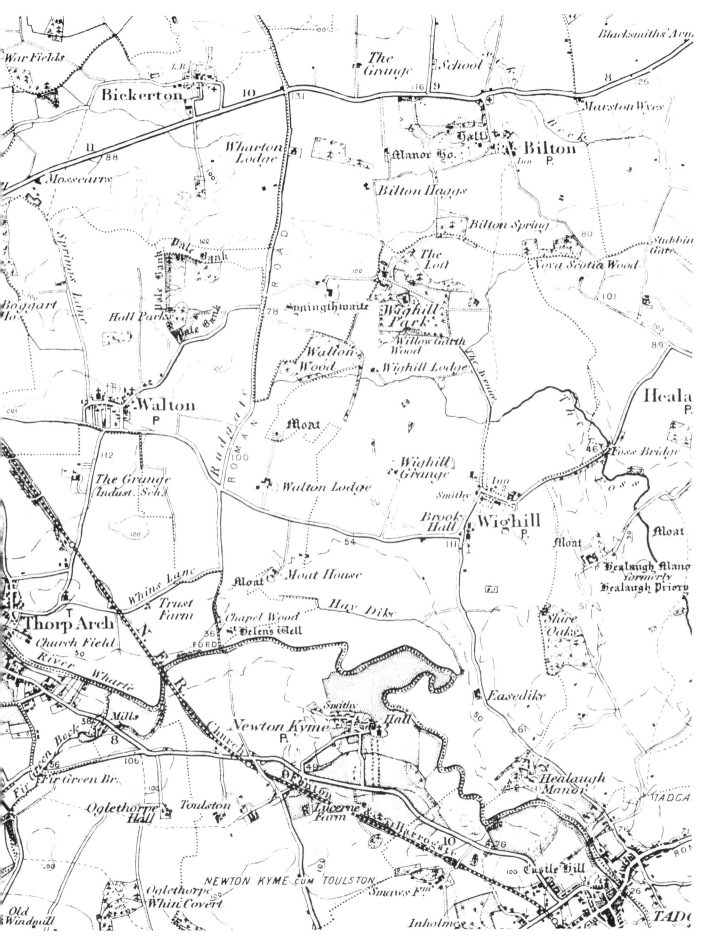

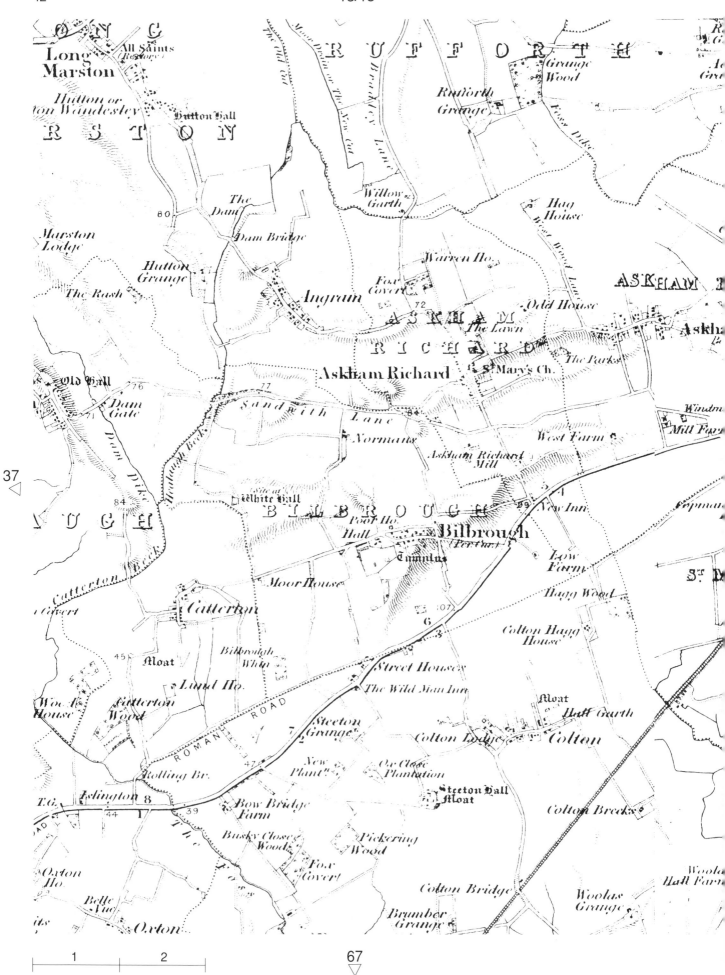

37

1   2

1 mile approx.

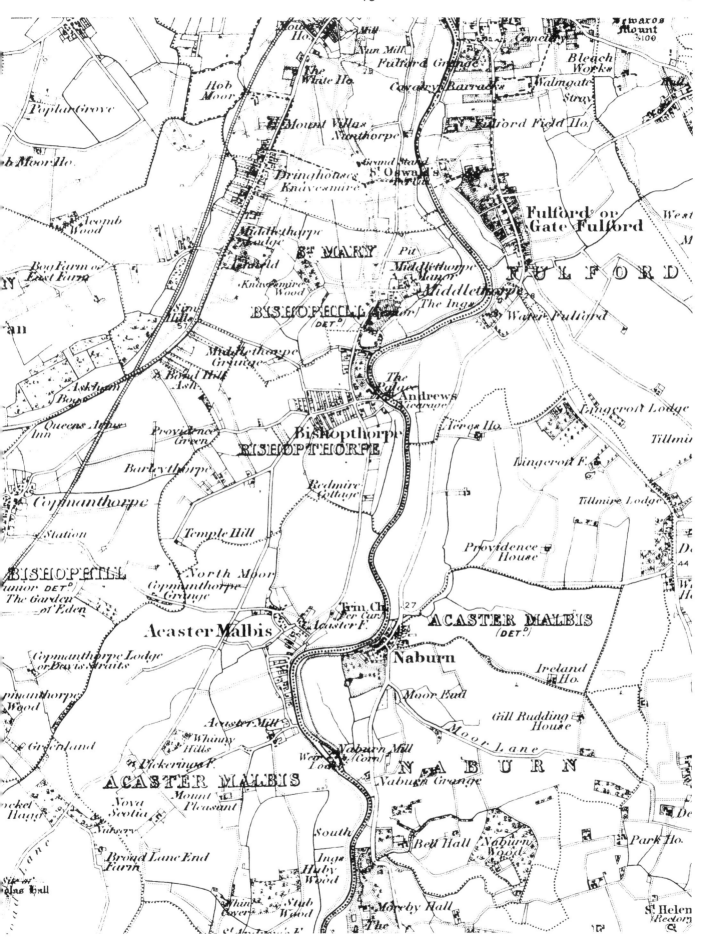

Published 1858.

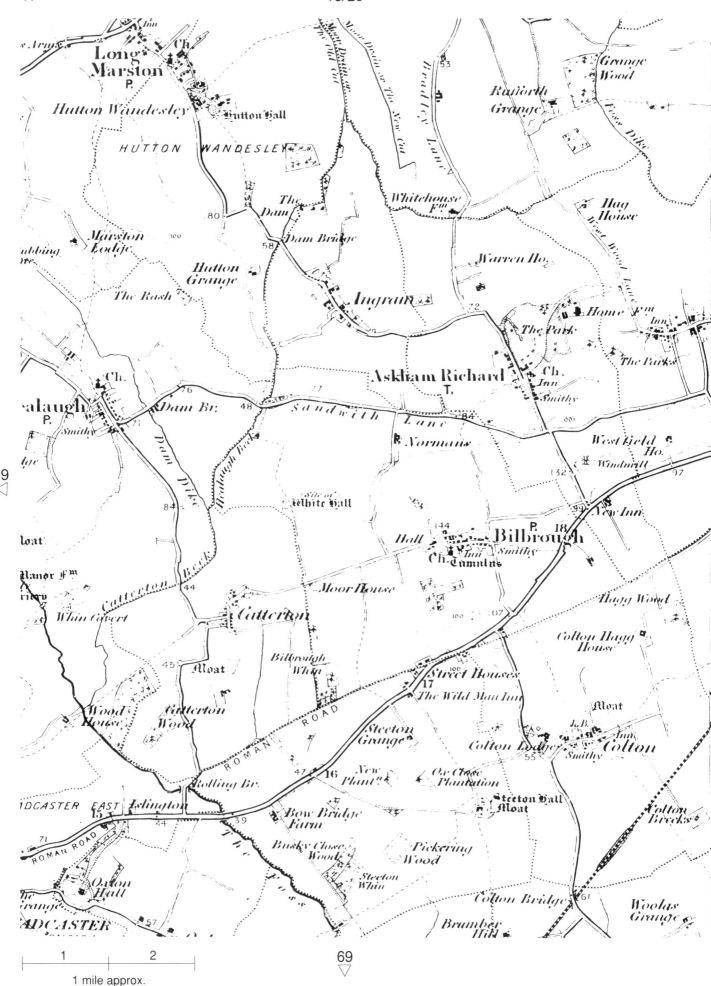

39

Long Marston
P.
Hutton Wandesley
Hutton Hall
HUTTON WANDESLEY
Marston Lodge
The Dam
Dam Bridge
80
58
Hutton Grange
The Rash
Whitehouse Fm
Bradley Lane
Rufforth Grange
Grange Wood
Foss Dike
West Wood Lane
Hag House
53
Warren Ho.
Ingram
72
The Park
Home Fm
Inn
The Parks
Askham Richard
T.
Ch.
Inn
Smithy
ealaugh
P.
Ch.
Smithy
Dam Br.
48
76
Sandwith Lane
84
601
Normans
Westfield Ho.
132
Windmill
97
New Inn
99
Healaugh Beck
Dam Dike
84
Site of White Hall
Hall
144
P.
Bilbrough
18
Manor Fm
iew
oat
Catterton Beck
44
Ch. Tumulus
Inn
Smithy
Whin Covert
Moor House
100
107
Hagg Wood
Catterton
Colton Hagg House
45
Moat
Bilbrough Whin
Street Houses
17
The Wild Man Inn
Moat
Wood House
Catterton Wood
ROMAN ROAD
Steeton Grange
New Plant?
Ox Close Plantation
Colton Lodge
55
Inn
Smithy
Colton
47
16
Rolling Br.
Bow Bridge Farm
Steeton Hall Moat
Colton Breckes
NDCASTER
EAST
Islington
15
44
39
ROMAN ROAD
71
Busky Close Wood
The Foss
Pickering Wood
Steeton Whin
Colton Bridge
61
Woolas Grange
Oxton Hall
57
Brumber Hill

1   2

1 mile approx.

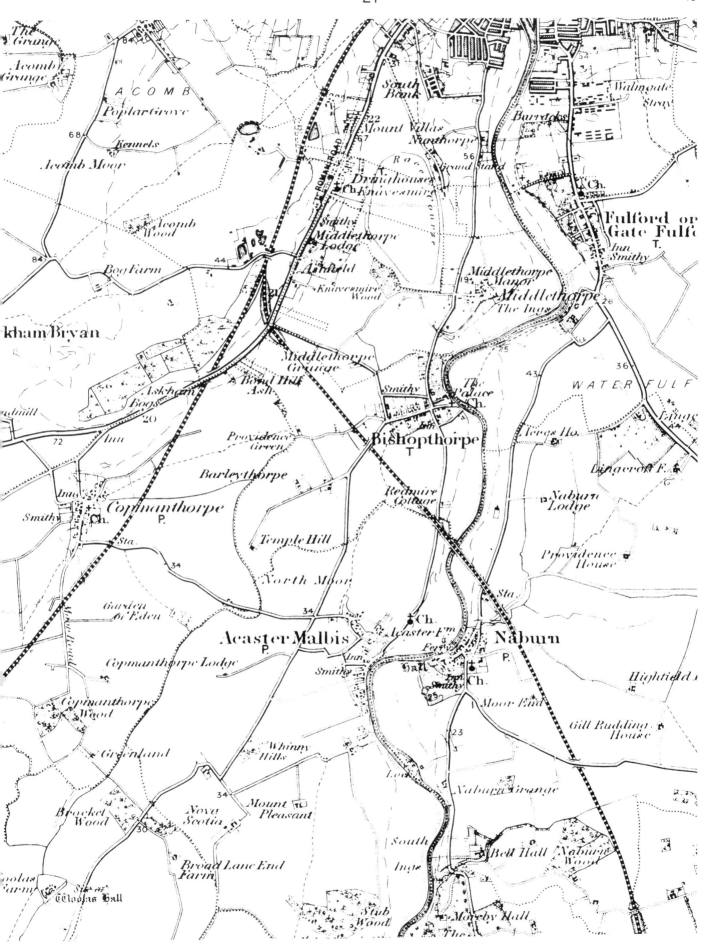

Surveyed 1843 - 49. Revised 1896. Published 1898 - 99.

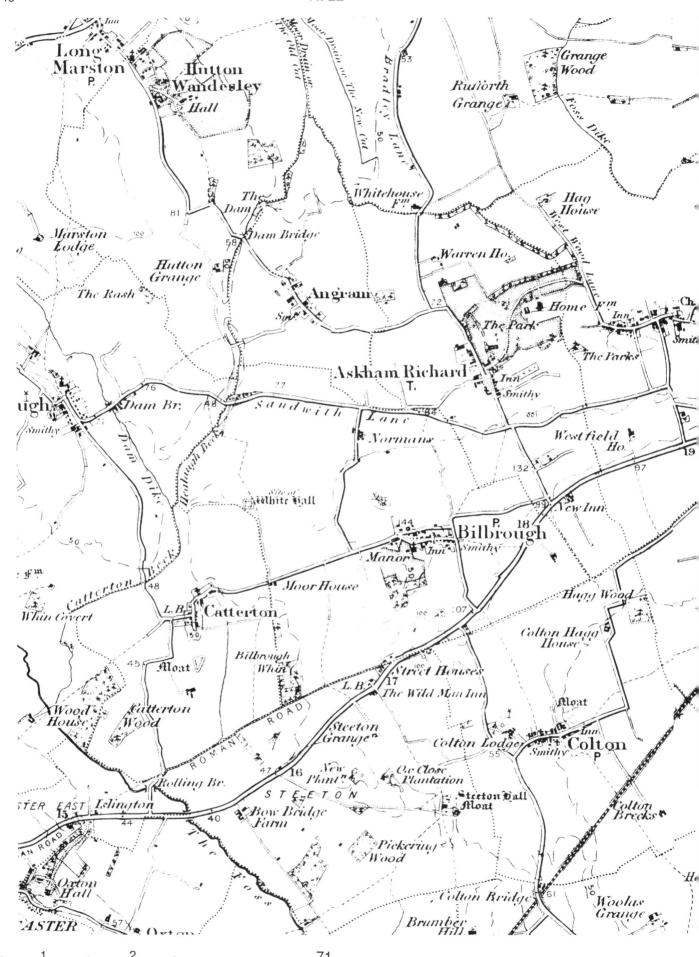

1 mile approx.

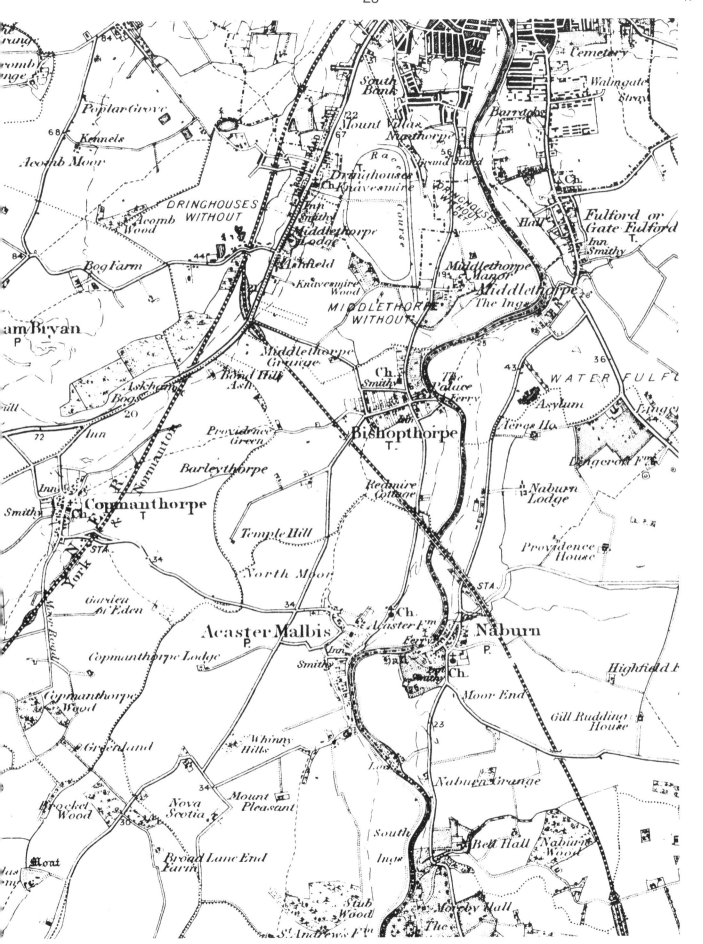

Surveyed 1843 - 49. Revised 1910. Published 1913.

1   2

1 mile approx.

Published 1858.

1   2

1 mile approx.

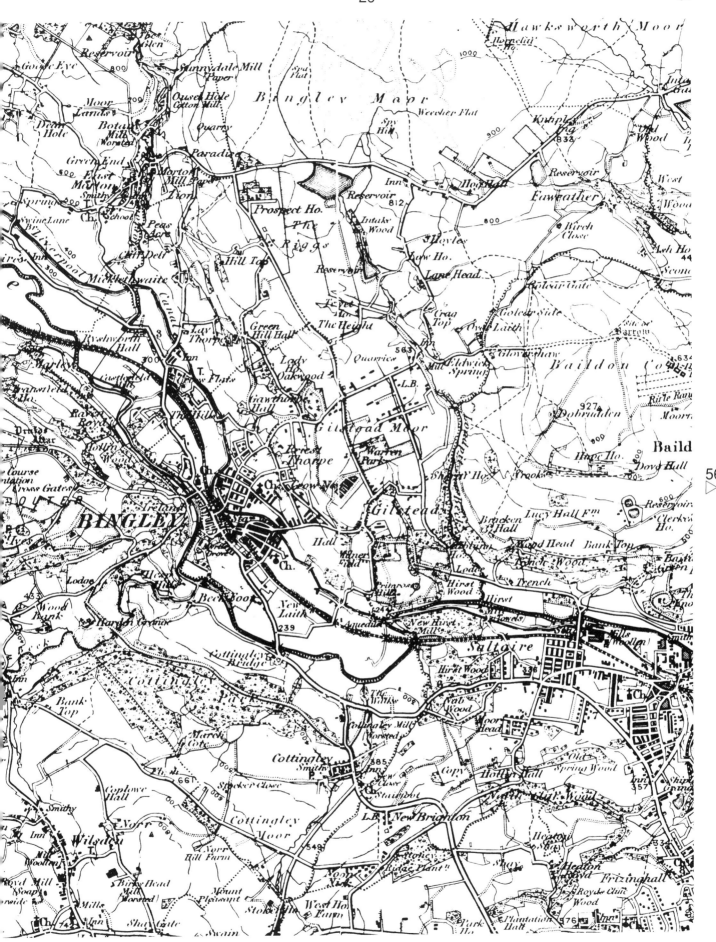

75/80 Surveyed 1843 - 49. Revised 1896. Published 1898 - 99.

1 | 2

1 mile approx.

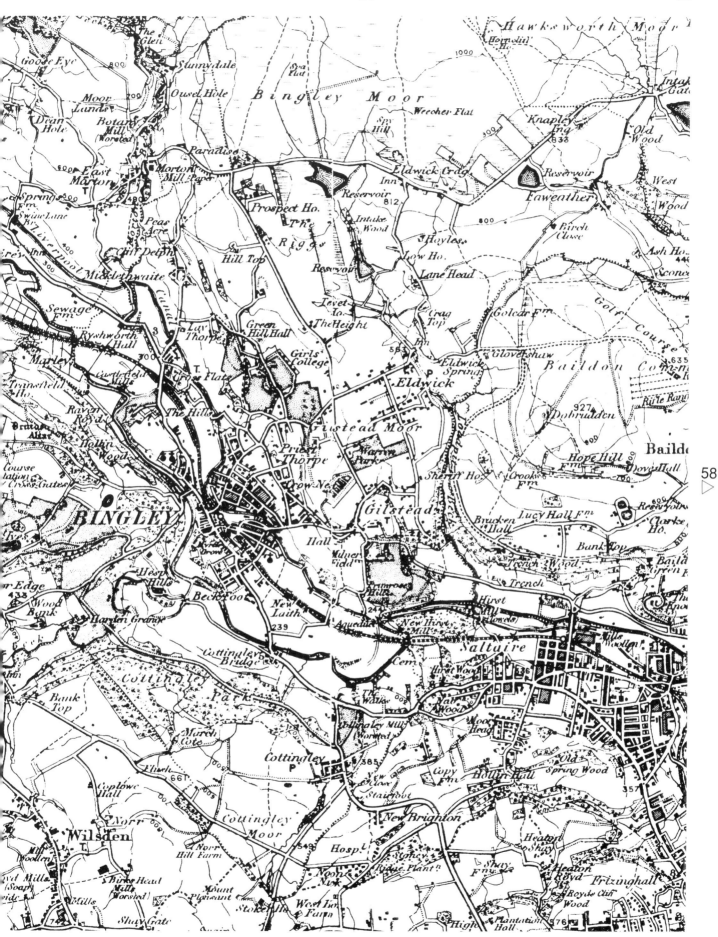

Surveyed 1843 - 49. Revised 1910. Published 1913.

1   2

1 mile approx.

Published 1858.

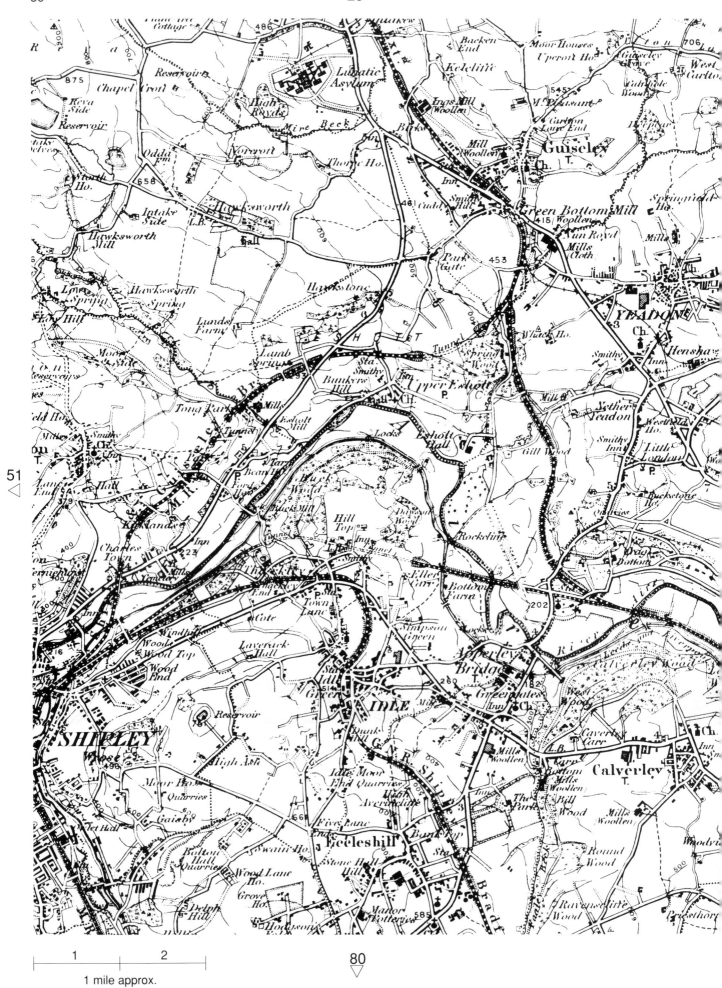

1 mile approx.

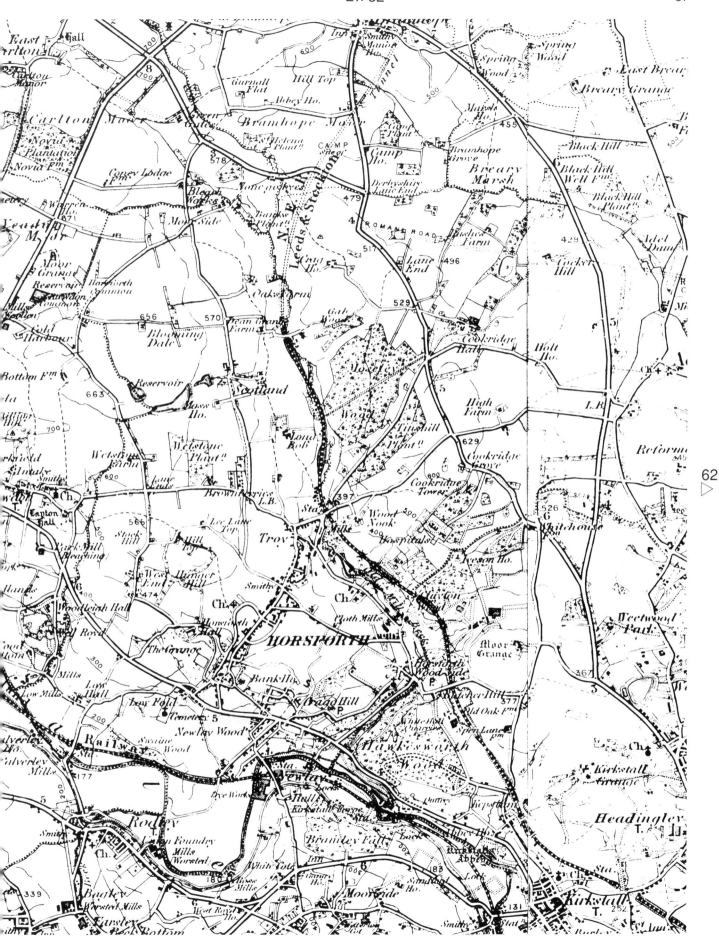

Reva Hill
Plane Tree Cottage
Intakes
Backen End
Moor Houses
Uproft Ho.
707
Guiseley Grove
West Carlton
Reservoir
Lunatic Asylum
Kelcliffe
545
Mt Pleasant
Reva Side
875
High Royds
Ings Mill Woollen
Carlton Lane End
Deipkier
Reservoir
Odda Fm
Norcroft
Mire Beck
Inn
Mill Woollen
GUISELEY
658
Thorpe
461
Storth Ho.
Hawksworth
L.B.
415
Springfield Ho.
Intake Fm
Hawksworth Mill
Hall
Parks Gate
453
Mill Cloth
Golf Course
Hawkstone Fm
YEADON
8
Low Spring
Hawksworth Spring
E S H O L T
Whack Ho.
Henshaw
Low Hill
Lunds Farm
Tunnel
Spring Wood
Moor Side
Lamb Spring
293
Smithy Ho.
Upper Esholt
P
Nether Yeadon
Don Reservoirs
Beck
Br.
Bunkers Hill
Gill Wood
Little London
P
Tong Park
Mills
Lock
Esholt Hall
5
Buckstone Ho.
Mills
Park
Tarn
Sewage Wks
Bean Ho.
Buck Wood
Dawson Wood
Crag Battery
Hall
Ford Ho.
53
Kirkland
Charles Town
Inn
223
Tunnel
Tunnel
Rockcliffe
River
Leeds and Liverpool
Calverley Wood
490
Ellar Carr
Bottom Farm
Mills
Thackley
Charley End
Simpson Green
Apperley Bridge
West Royd
Sewage Wks
300
Town Lane
Cote
Locks
Greengates
Calverley Carr
Laverick Hall
286
Inn
Wood Top
Idle
32
Wood End
P
514
Mills
Bottom Mills Woollen
Bill Wood
SHIPLEY
Whose
490
Reservoir
High Ash
Dunk Hill
G.N.R. Ship
Mills Woollen
The Inn
Mills Woollen
Moor Ho.
Idle Moor
Elec. Tram.
Round Wood
Quarries
500
Gaisby
66
Five Lane Ends
Path Stop
Woodvil
Orlet Hall
Bolton Hall
Swain Ho.
Eccleshill
Ravenscliffe Wood
Priesthorp
Wood Lane Ho.
Manor Potteries
585
L.B.
Delf Hill
Grove Ho.
Hodgson's

1 mile approx.

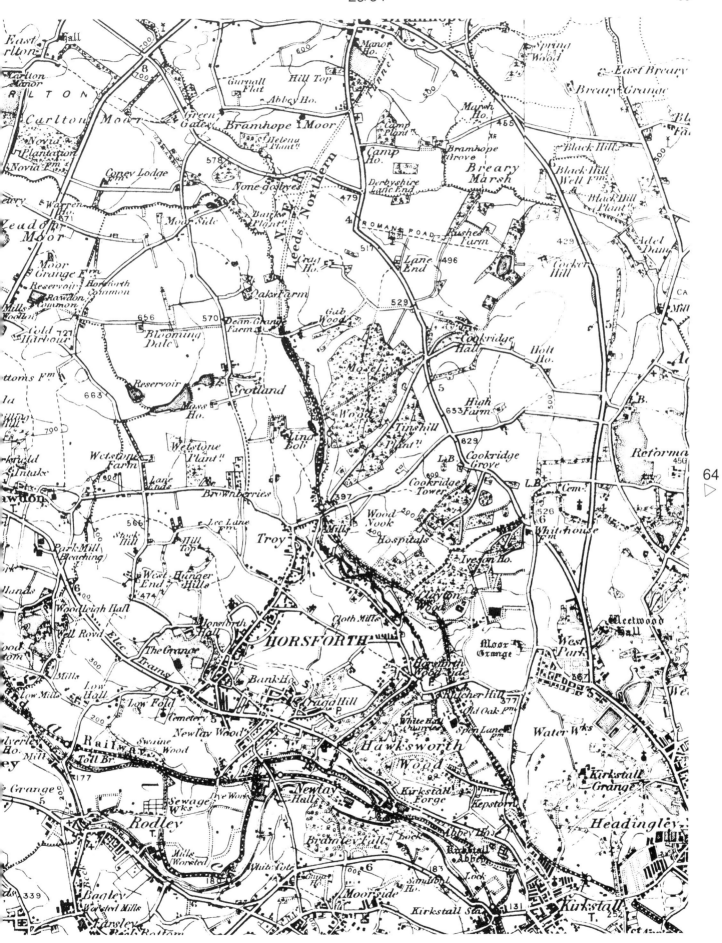

Surveyed 1843 - 49. Revised 1910. Published 1913.

55

1   2

1 mile approx.

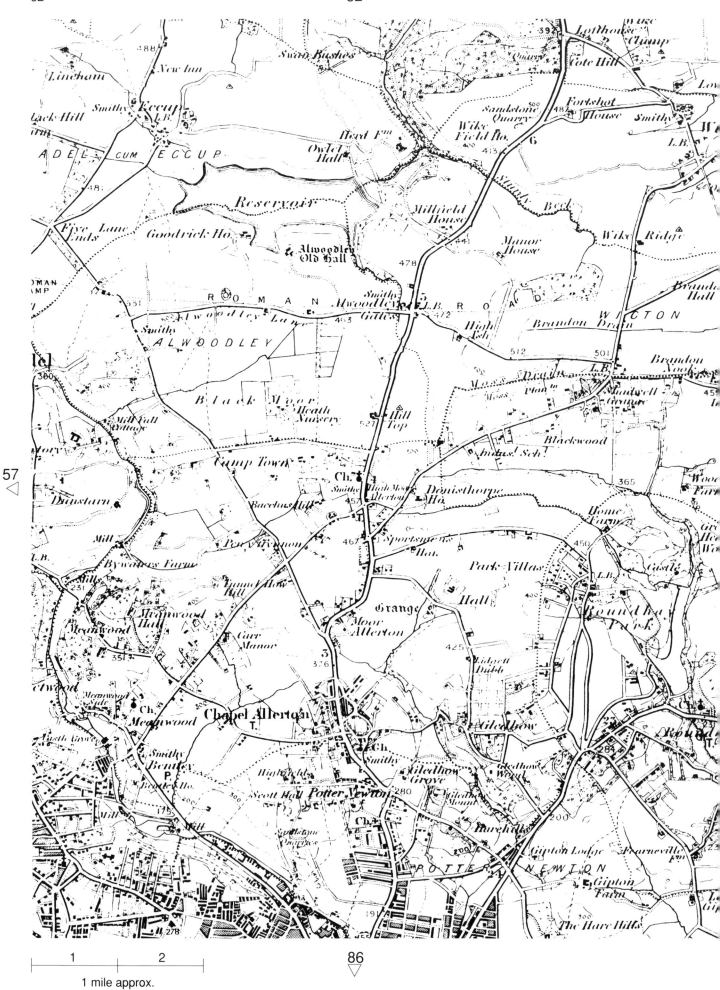

1   2

1 mile approx.

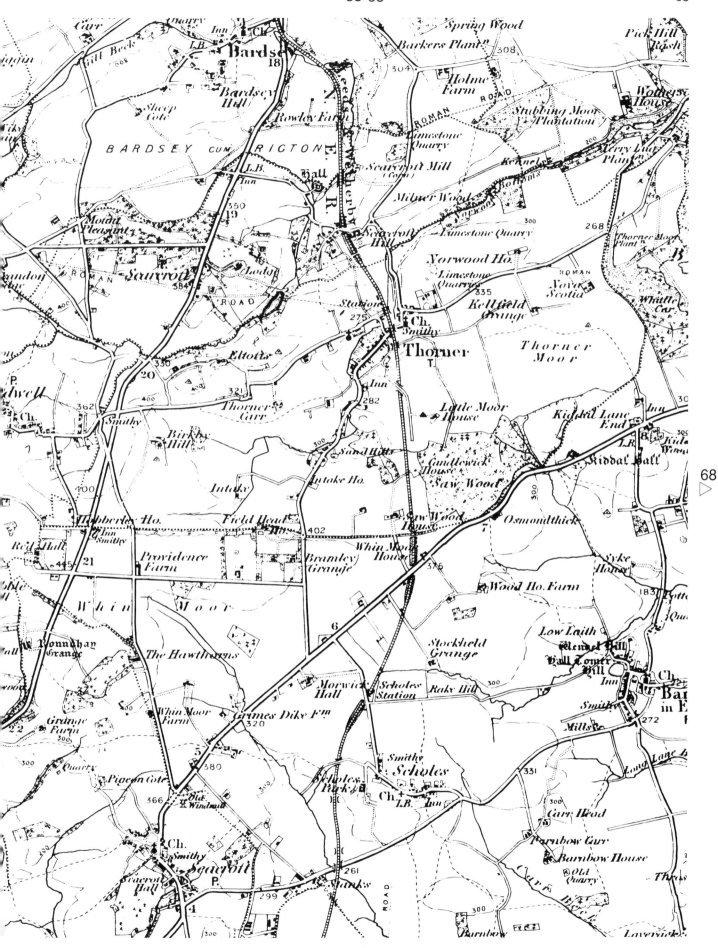

Surveyed 1843 - 47. Revised 1896. Published 1898.

Lofthouse
Swan Bushes
Cote Hill
Lineham Fm
Smithy Eccup
Black Hill
Herd Fm
Owlet Hall
Wike Field Ho.
Fortshot House
Smith
Wik
ADEL CUM ECCUP
Reservoir
Millfield House
Manor House
Wike Ridge
Five Lane Ends
Goodrick Ho.
Alwoodley Old Hall
Brandon Hall
ROMAN
Alwoodley Lane
Smith
Golf Course
WICTON
Brandon Drain
ALWOODLEY
High Ash
Slaid Hill
Black Moor
Golf Course
Heath Nursery
Hill Top
Shadwell Grange
Blackwood
Mill Fall Cottage
Camp Town
Indus. Sch.
Dunstarn Fm
Manor Ho.
Donisthorpe Ho.
Moor Allerton
Park Villas
Mill
Pen y Mynnon
Bywatery Farm
Tunnel How Hill
Grange
Hall
Roundhay Park
Meanwood Hall
Carr Manor
Lidget Park
Chapel Allerton
Gledhow
Meanwood
Bentley
Gledhow Grove
Harehill
Scott Hall
Old Windmill
Gipton Lodge
Fearnevill
Mill
Quarries
Gipton Farm

1
2
1 mile approx.

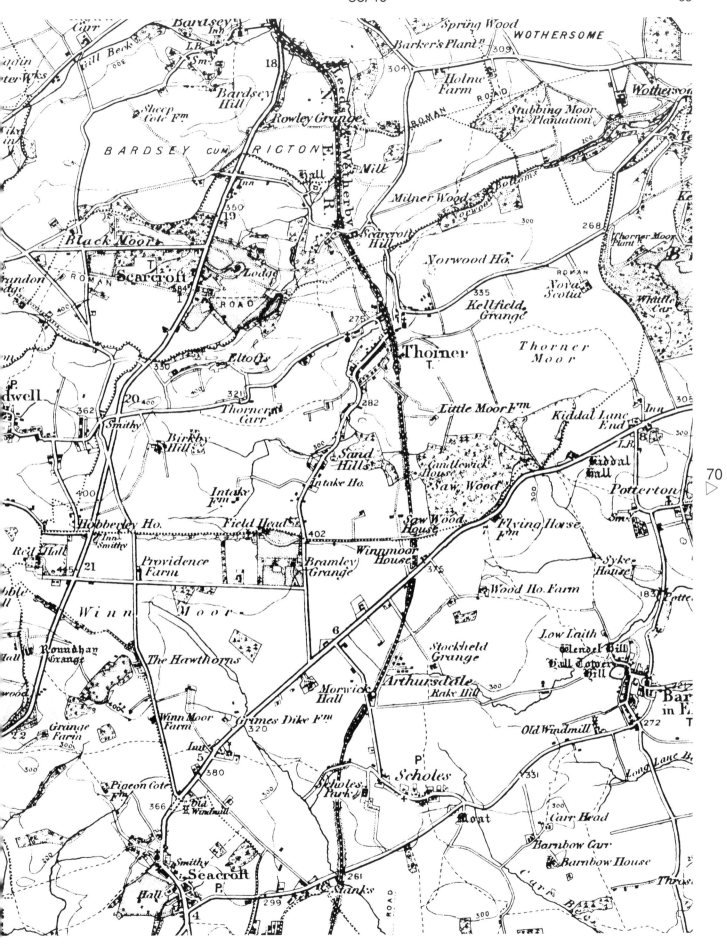

1   2

1 mile approx.

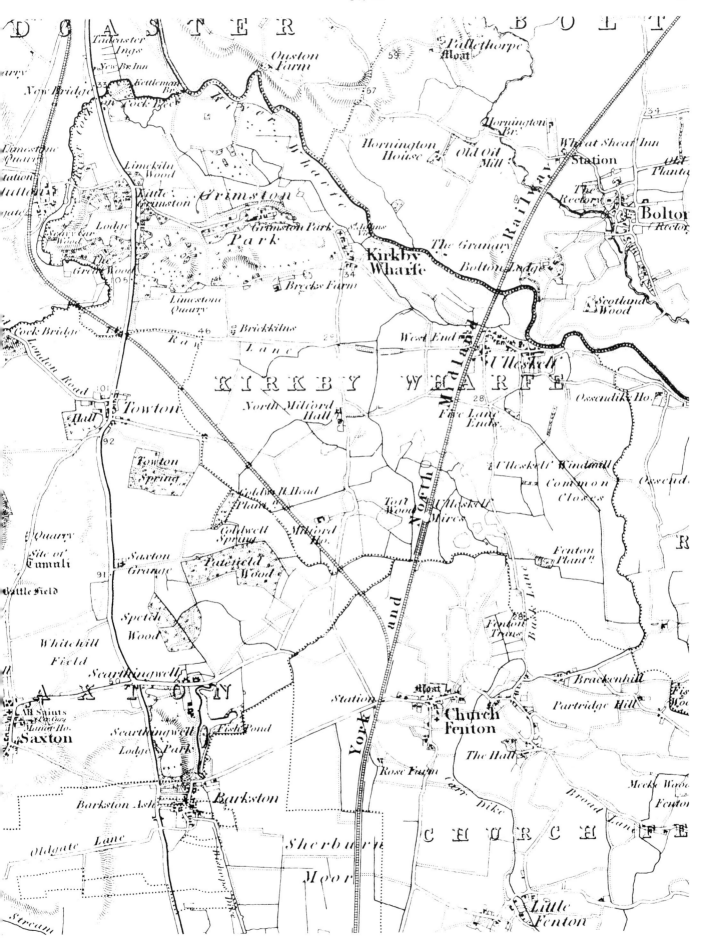

Published 1858.

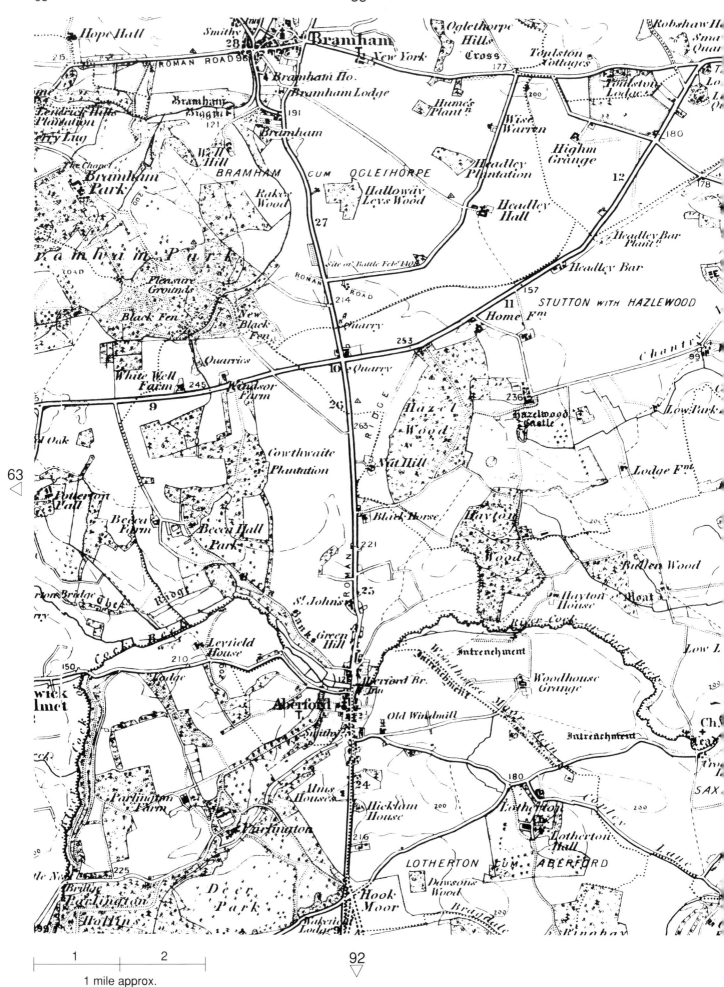

Hope Hall
Smithy
28
Bramham
New York
Oglethorpe Hill.
Cross
Toulston Cottages
Robshaw
Sma
Qua

ROMAN ROAD 96
Bramham Ho.
177
Toulston Lodge

215
Bramham Lodge
200
180

Bramham Biggin
121
191
Hume's Plant.
Wise Warren
Highm Grange
12
178

Teidrich Hills Plantation
Bramham
Wall Hill
BRAMHAM CUM OGLETHORPE
Raker Wood
Halloway Leys Wood
Headley Plantation
Headley Hall
Headley Bar Plant.

The Chapel
Bramham Park
27
Site of Battle Feb. 1408
ROMAN ROAD
214
Headley Bar
157
11
STUTTON WITH HAZLEWOOD

Bramham Park
ROAD
Pleasure Grounds
Home Fm.

Black Fen
New Black Fen
Quarry
253
Hazel Wood
Hazelwood Castle
236
Low Park

Quarries
10 Quarry
RIDGE
263
Lodge Fm.

White Well Farm
245
Windsor Farm
26
Nut Hill
220

9
Cowthwaite Plantation
221
Black Horse
Hayton Wood
Radlen Wood

Oak
Potterton Hall
Becca Farm
Becca Hall Park
Hayton Moat House
River Cock or Cock B

ton Bridge Cock
Ridge
Beck
25
St. Johns
Bank Green Hill
Intrenchment
Woodhouse Moor
Intrenchment
Low

150
Leyfield House
210
Lodge
Aberford Br.
Woodhouse Grange
Ch.
Saх

wick Elmet
Aberford
T
Old Windmill
Intrenchment

Smithy
24
Parlington Farm
Mus House
Hicklam House
200
180
Lotherton
Copley
200

Parlington
216
Lotherton Hall
Lotherton Lane

Deer Park
225
Hollins
Hook Moor
Dawsons Wood
LOTHERTON CUM ABERFORD
Bragdale
Ringhay

de No
Bridge Parlington

1
2
1 mile approx.

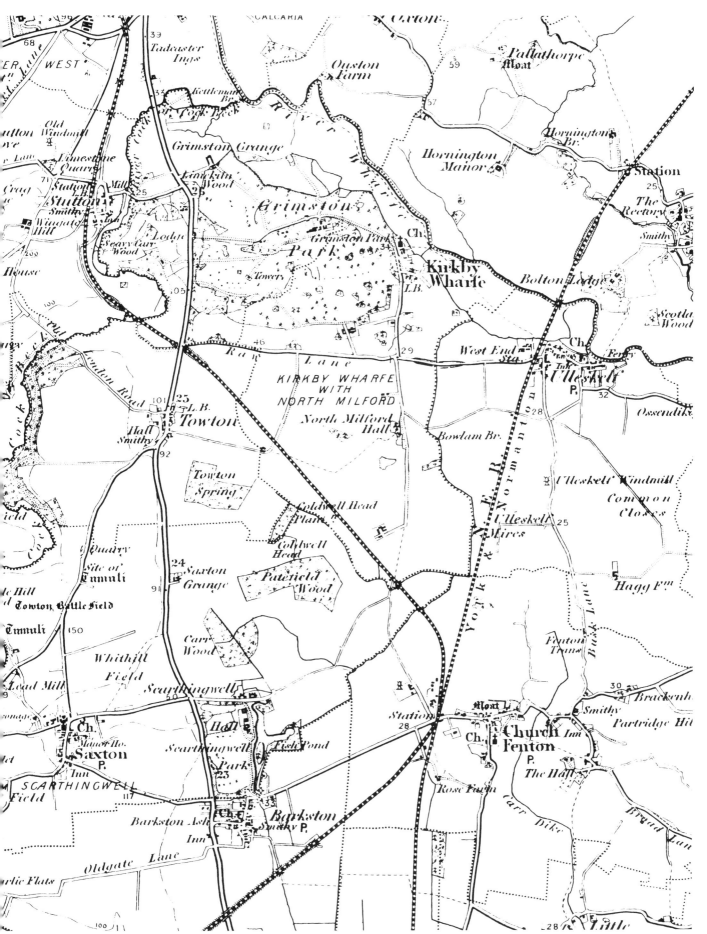

Surveyed 1843 - 47. Revised 1896. Published 1898.

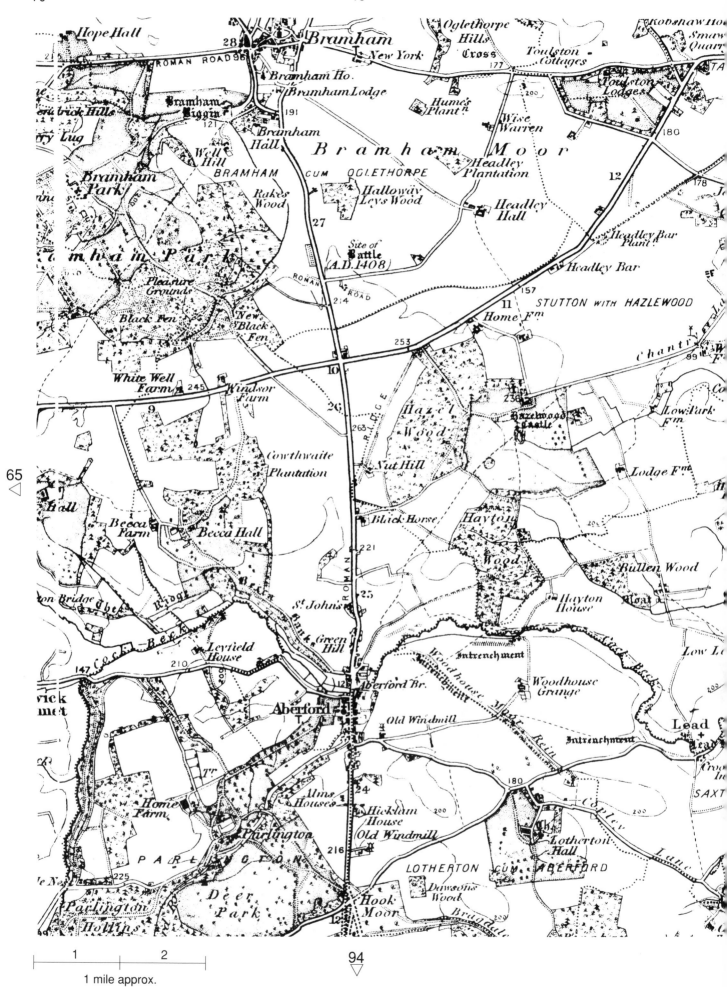

Hope Hall

28

ROMAN ROAD

Bramham

New York

Oglethorpe Hills

Cross

Toulston Cottages

Robshaw Ho

Small Quarr

TA

Bramham Ho.

Bramham Lodge

Hume's Plant.

177

Wise Warren

Toulston Lodge

Bramham Biggin

121

191

Bramham Hall

Well Hill

BRAMHAM CUM OGLETHORPE

Bramham Park

cramham Park

Pleasure Grounds

Black Fen

New Black Fen

White Well Farm

Windsor Farm

9

245

Cowthwaite Plantation

Hall

Becca Farm

Becca Hall

on Bridge

The Ridge

Leyfield House

147

wick met

Home Farm

Parlington

PARLINGTON

Ne

225

Parlington Hollins

Deer Park

Bramham Moor

Headley Plantation

Halloway Leys Wood

Rakes Wood

27

Site of Battle (A.D. 1408)

ROMAN ROAD

214

10

26

263

RIDGE

221

St. John's

Green Hill

ROMAN

25

Aberford Br.

Aberford

Old Windmill

Alms Houses

24

Hickham House (Old Windmill)

216

Black Horse

Nut Hill

Headley Hall

Headley Bar Plant.

Headley Bar

157

11

Home Fm

253

12

178

200

180

Je

STUTTON WITH HAZLEWOOD

Hazel Wood

256

Hazelwood Castle

Hayton Wood

Hayton House

Woodhouse Moor

Intrenchment

Woodhouse Grange

Intrenchment

Chantr

99

Low Park Fm

Lodge Fm

Co

Bullen Wood

Goat

Low Lo

180

Copler

200

Lane

Lead

Cro

SAXT

Lotherton Hall

LOTHERTON CUM ABERFORD

Hook Moor

Dawsons Wood

Bragdale

94

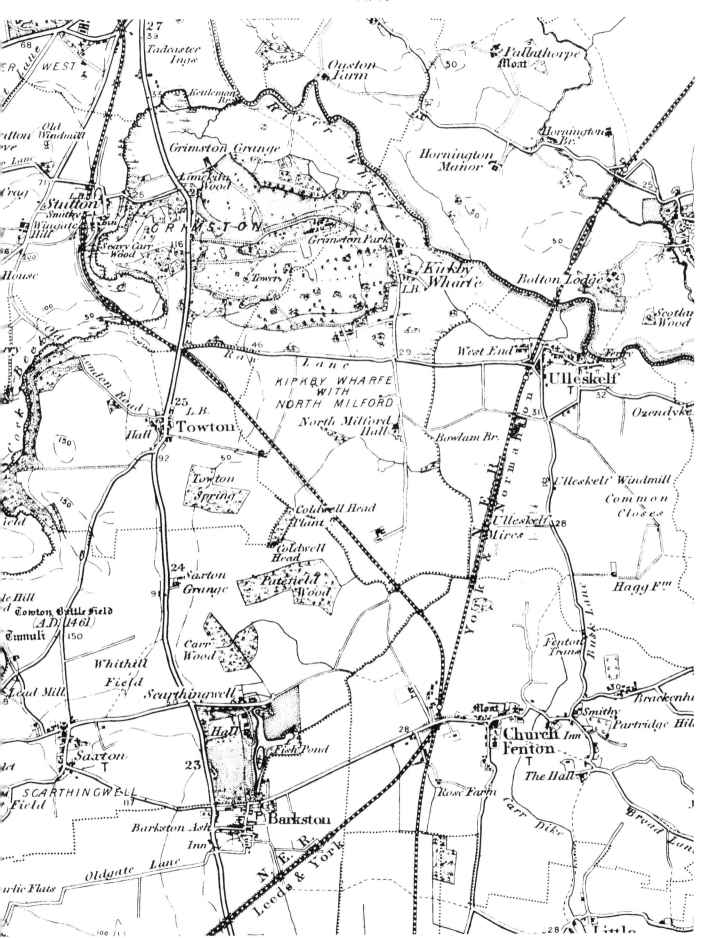

Surveyed 1843 - 49. Revised 1910. Published 1913.

1

2

1 mile approx.

Published 1842 - 44.

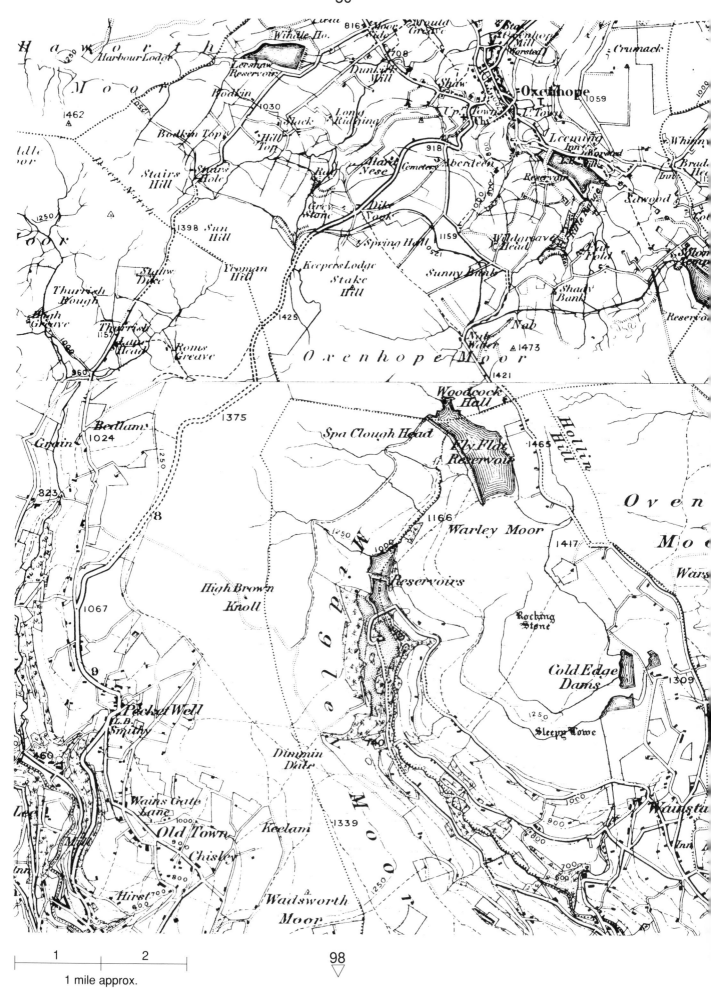

1   2

1 mile approx.

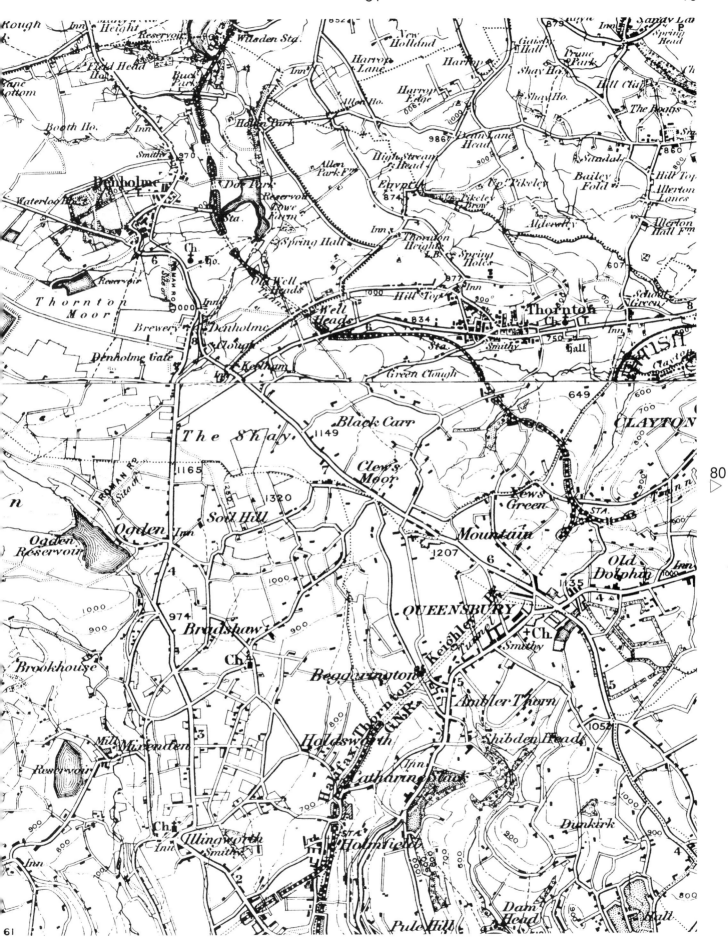

99 Surveyed 1843 - 49 / 1871 - 72. Revised 1894. Published 1896.

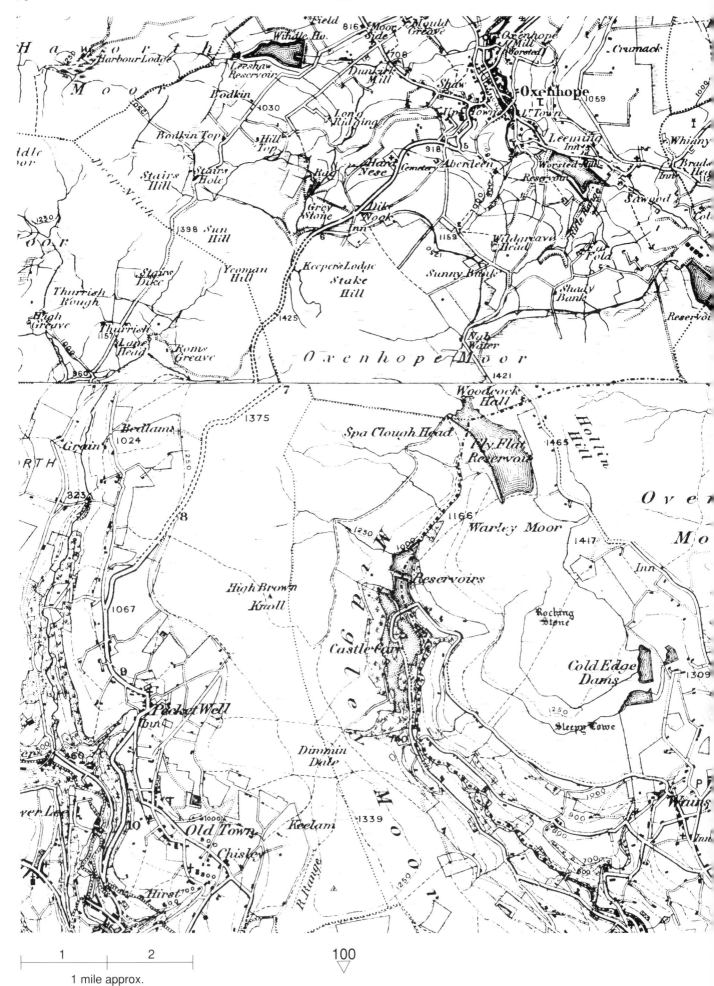

1   2

1 mile approx.

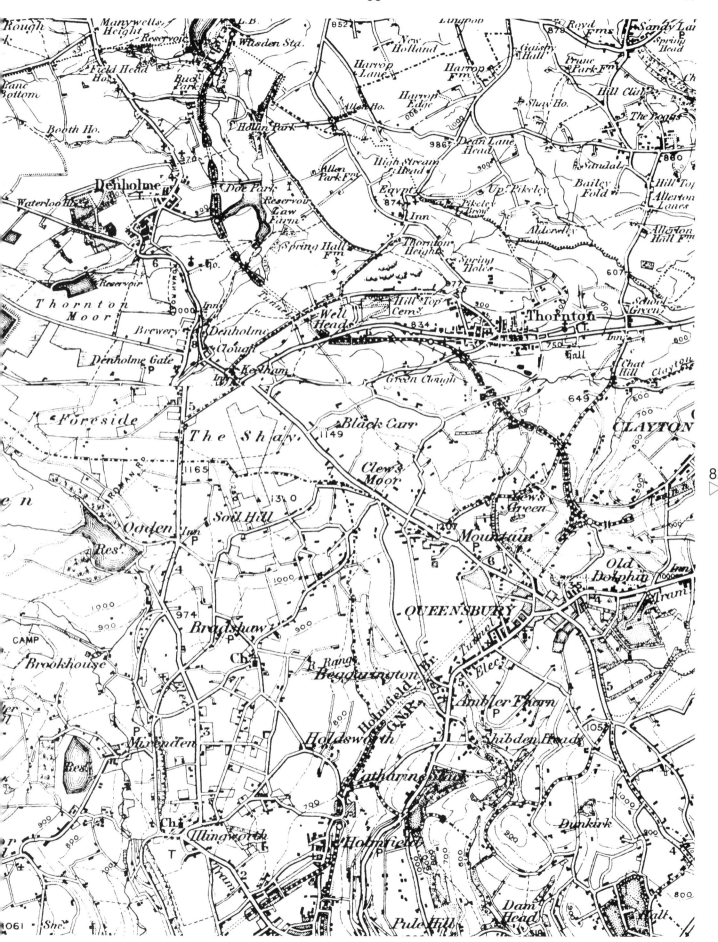

Surveyed 1843 - 49 / 1887 - 93. Revised 1908 - 10. Published 1911 - 13.

Published 1842 - 44.

1 mile approx.

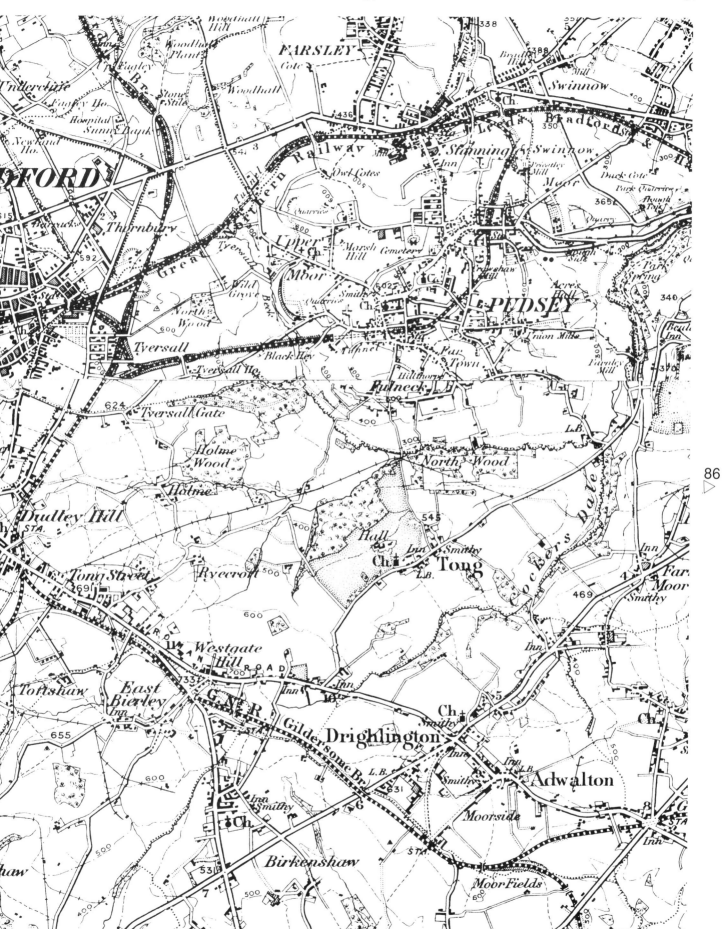

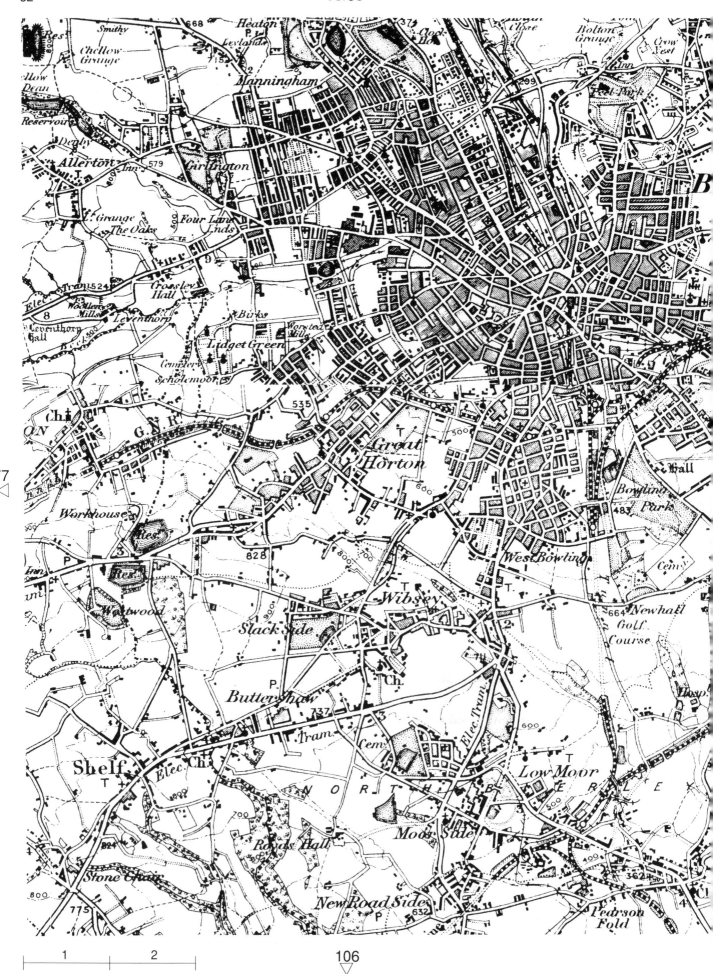

1 mile approx.

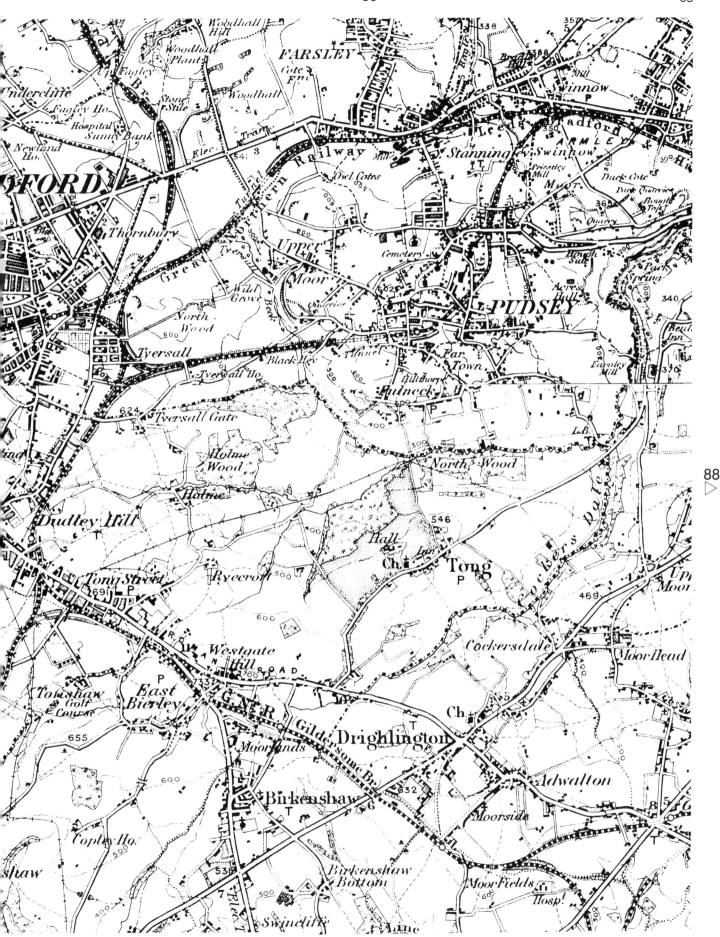

Surveyed 1843 - 49 / 1887 - 93. Revised 1908 - 10. Published 1911 - 13.

1 mile approx.

Published 1842 - 44.

1   2

1 mile approx.

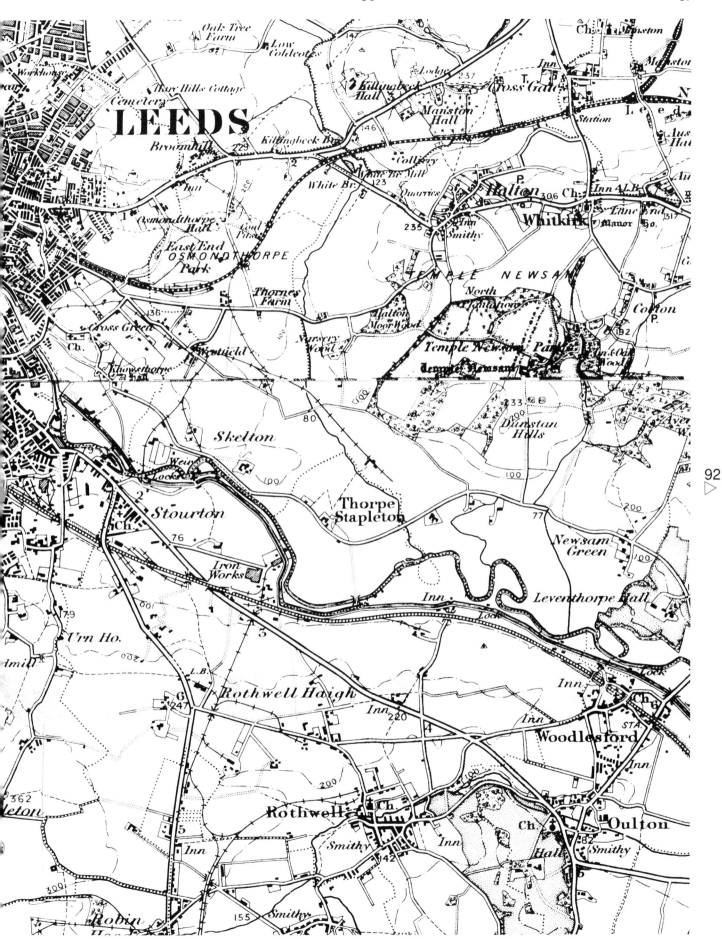

111   Surveyed 1843 - 49 / 1889 - 92. Revised 1894 - 96. Published 1896 - 99.

MORLEY

1 2

1 mile approx.

1   2

1 mile approx.

Published 1842 - 44.

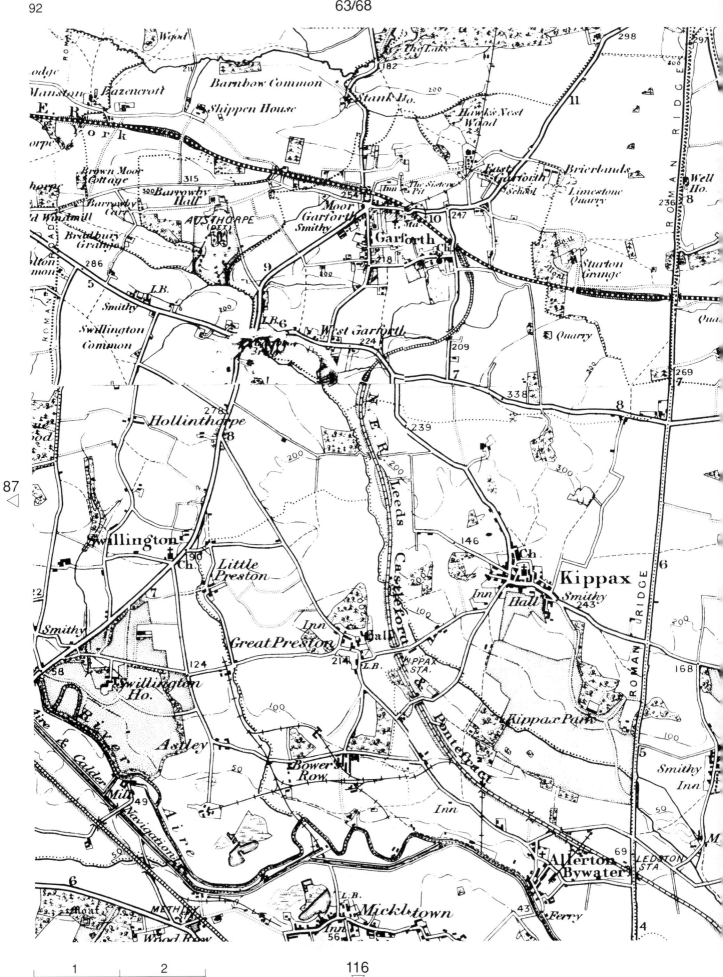

1 mile approx.

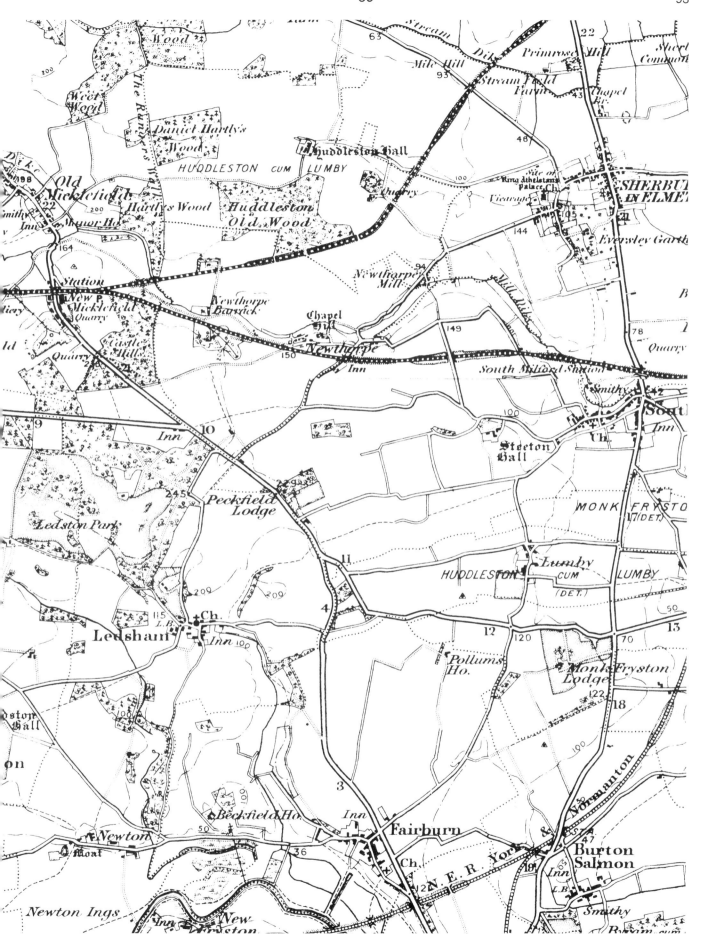

Surveyed 1843 - 49 / 1889 - 92. Revised 1894 - 96. Published 1896 - 99.

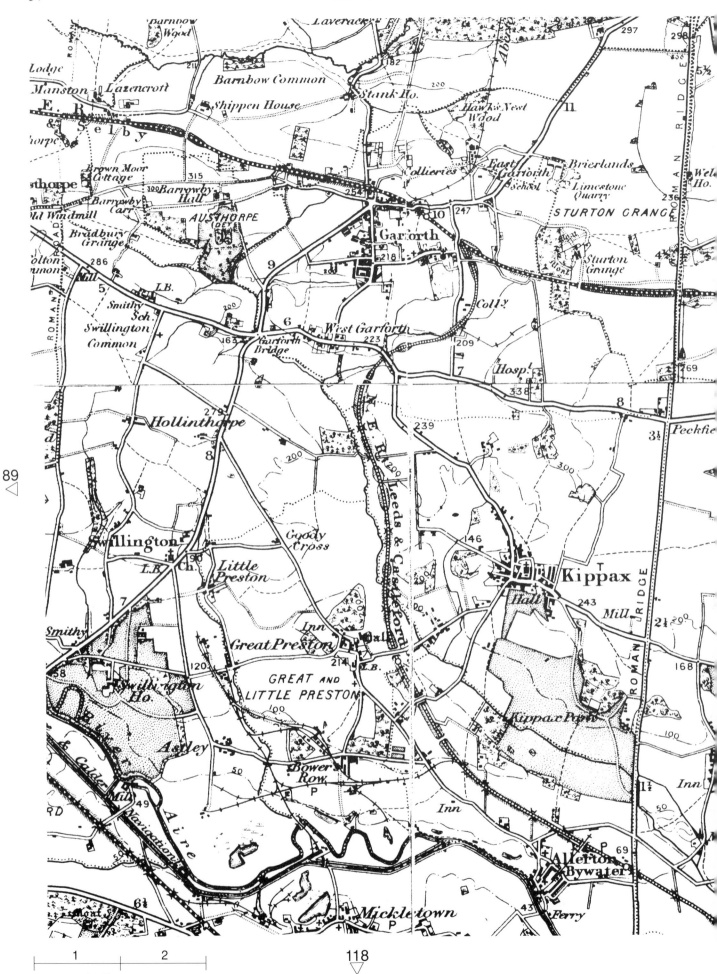

89

1   2

1 mile approx.

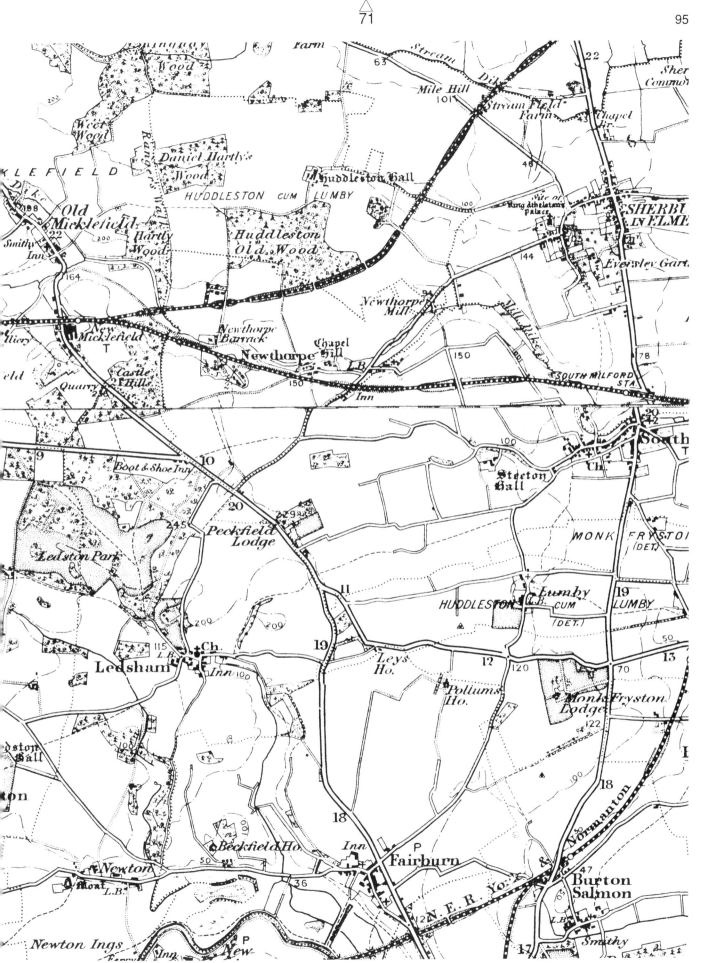

Surveyed 1843 - 49 / 1888 - 92. Revised 1908. Published 1911.

1 | 2

1 mile approx.

Published 1841.

HEBDEN BRIDGE

Booth

Broad

Midgley

Inn

L.B.

517

Luddende

Rochdale Canal

Wadsworth
Banks
Fields

Mytholmroyd

Inn

Old
Chamber

307

Smithy

6

324

Brearley

978

Ingden
range

Ch.

300

Halt Bank

Ch.

295

Luddenden
Foot

Hoo
Hole

Erringden
Moor

900

700

600

380

400

600

ST.

Ch.

Ho

Brantom

Bell Houses
Moor

Bridge Brook

1071

800

900

1000

River Ca

Blackwood
Common

Inn

Aaron
Hill

Long Edge
Moor

Smithy

ch. Sower

Rooley
Hill

Brockwell
Ho

Cragg

615

Ch.

Inn

High Stones
Hill

Red Brink

677

10

Smithy

700

800

900

1000

Crow Hill

1258

Cock Hill

1000

Toot Hill

900

1155

Triangle

373

Inn

Ch.

Inn

9

L.B.

Dean Ho.

963

Flints

Lumb
Mill Bank

800

Inn

Lebroyd

Clough

900

1000

Lighthazles

Soyland
Town

Great Manshead
Hill

743

Inn

8

Inn

1369

Ripponden

Ch.

1250

955

11

1

2

1 mile approx.

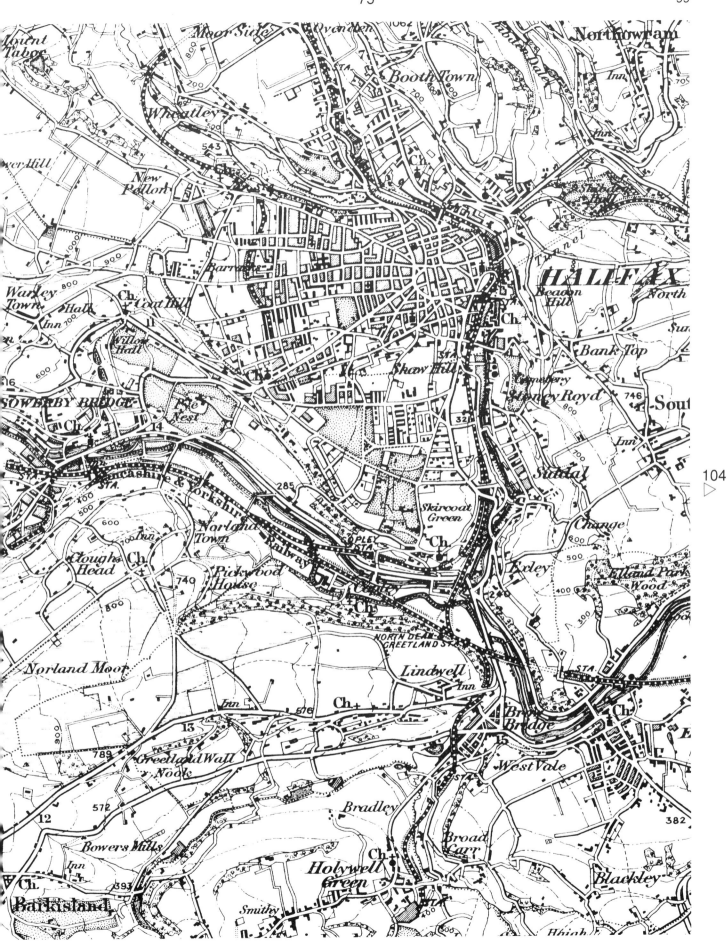

Surveyed 1871 - 72. Revised 1894. Published 1896.

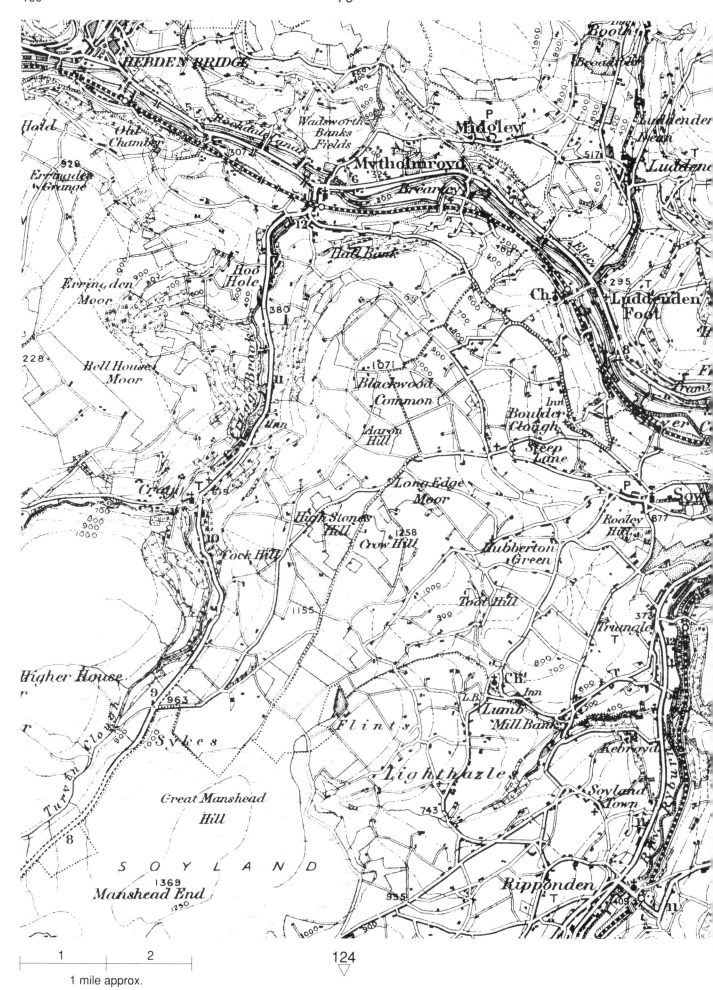

1 mile approx.

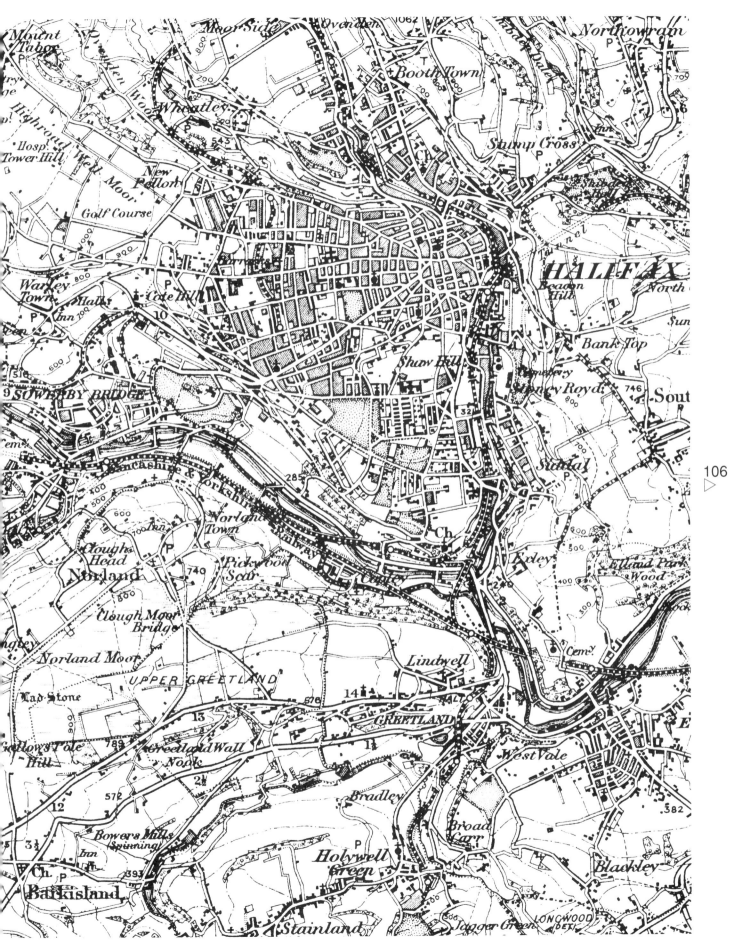

Surveyed 1887 - 93. Revised 1908. Published 1911.

1   2

1 mile approx.

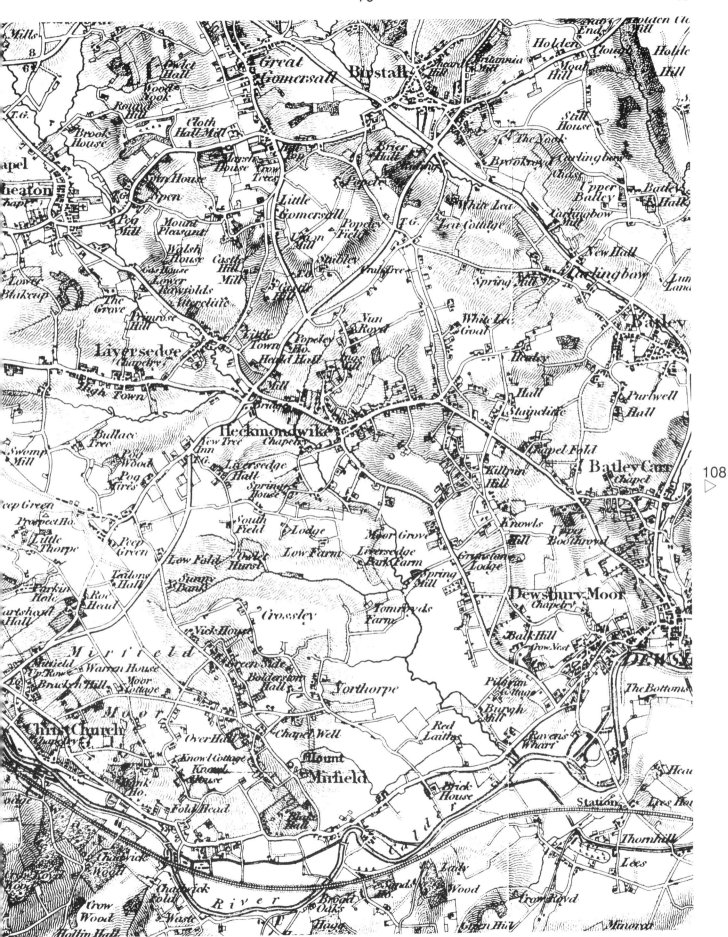

Published 1841.

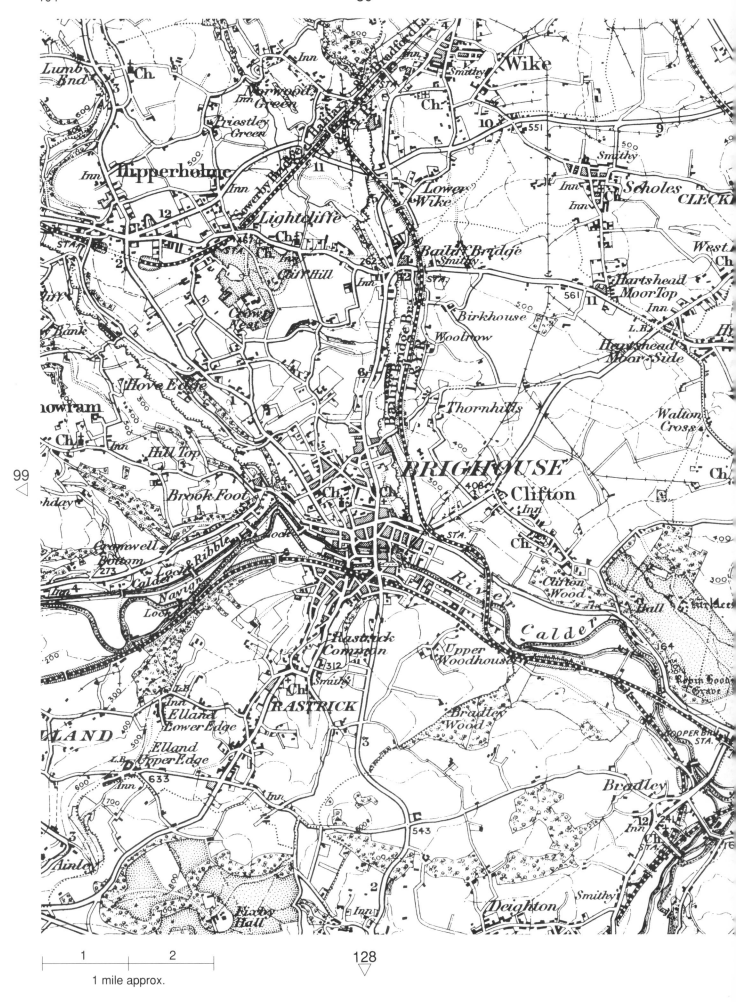

1   2

1 mile approx.

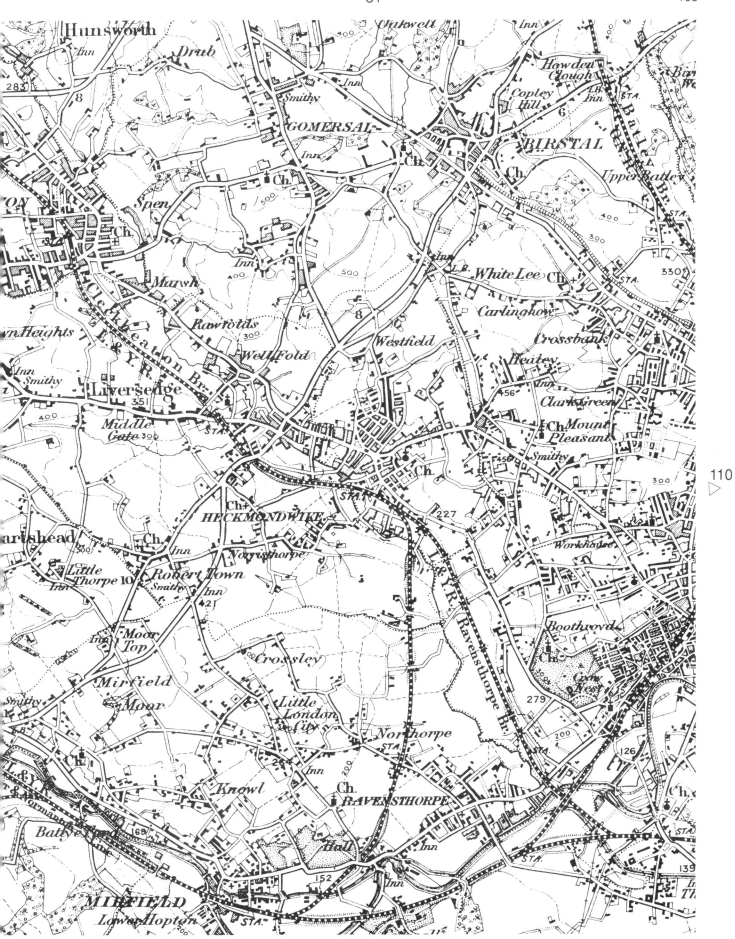

82
101

1   2

1 mile approx.

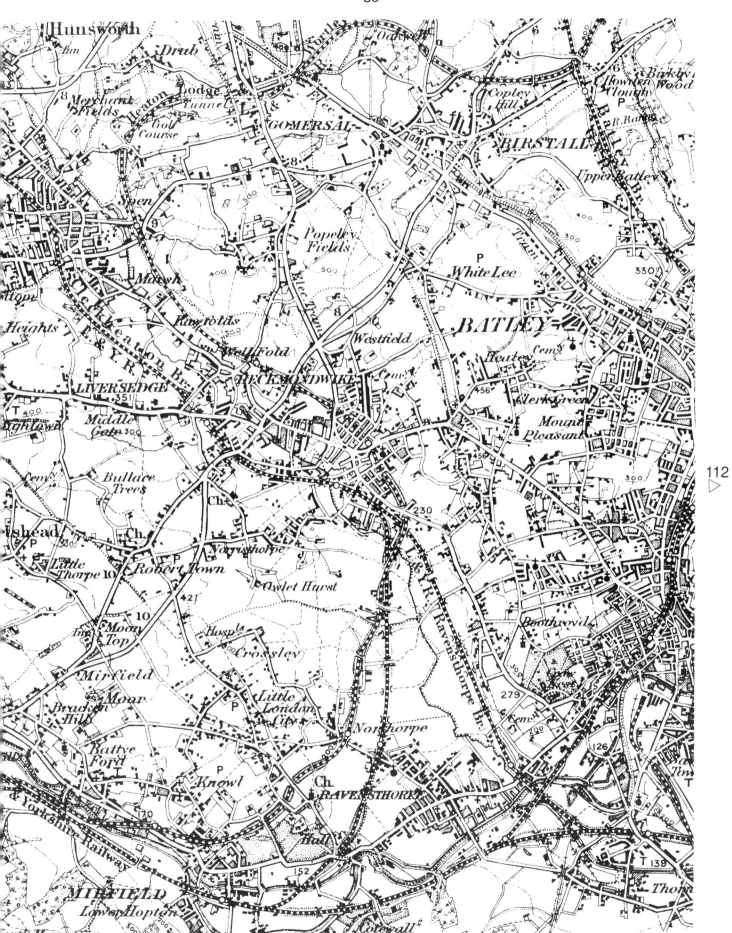

1 mile approx.

Published 1841.

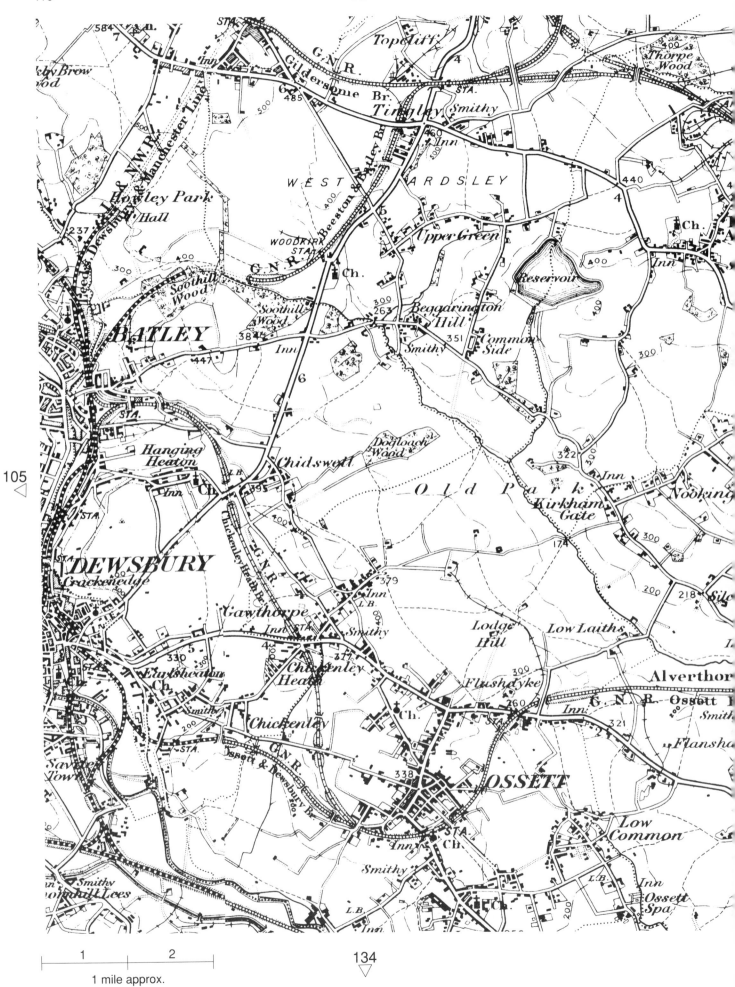

1   2

1 mile approx.

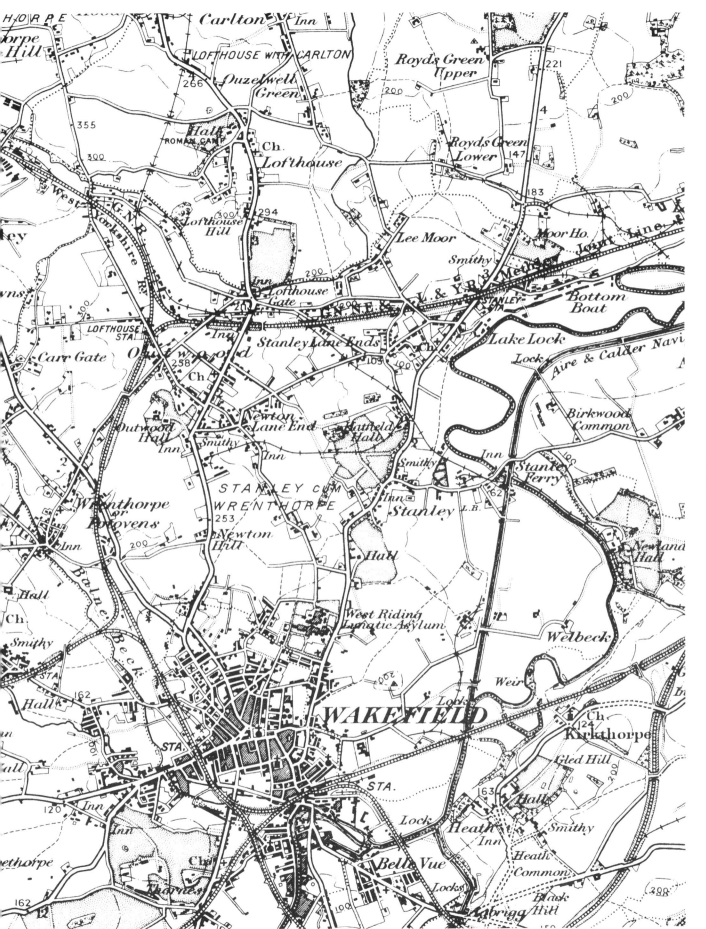

Surveyed 1889 - 92. Revised 1894. Published 1896.

584

Brow 500

G. N. R.

Topcliffe

Birks 485

Tingley

460

5

Iron Works

ARDSLEY WEST

439

4

Ch

Ards Ea

L & N W R & Manchester Line

Howley Park Hall

Dewsbury

238

300

G. N. R.

Woodkirk

Upper Green

Reservoir

400

La

3

300

Soothill Wood

Mill 263

Beggarington Hill

Common Side

351

300

384

Inn

300

Lower Soothill

447

6

Dogloitch Wood

Old Park

Beck Bottom

322

Inn

300

Hanging Heaton

Ch

Chidswell

Kirkham Gate

7

ALVERTHORPE

Batley Carr

200

218

Silcoates

DEWSBURY

379

Lodge

Low Laiths

Mill

rackenedge

Gawthorpe

4

Ossett Street Hill Side

Flushdyke

Earlsheaton

330

5

Chickenley Heath

300

3

Inn

G. N. R.

Ossett Br

SOOTHILL

NETHER

Chickenley

321

Shepherd Hill

Flanshaw

Hosp!

Ossett & Dewsbury

G. N. R.

338

OSSETT

2

200

Low Common

M R

ll Trees

Ossett Spa

LUPSE

Sna He

1   2

1 mile approx.

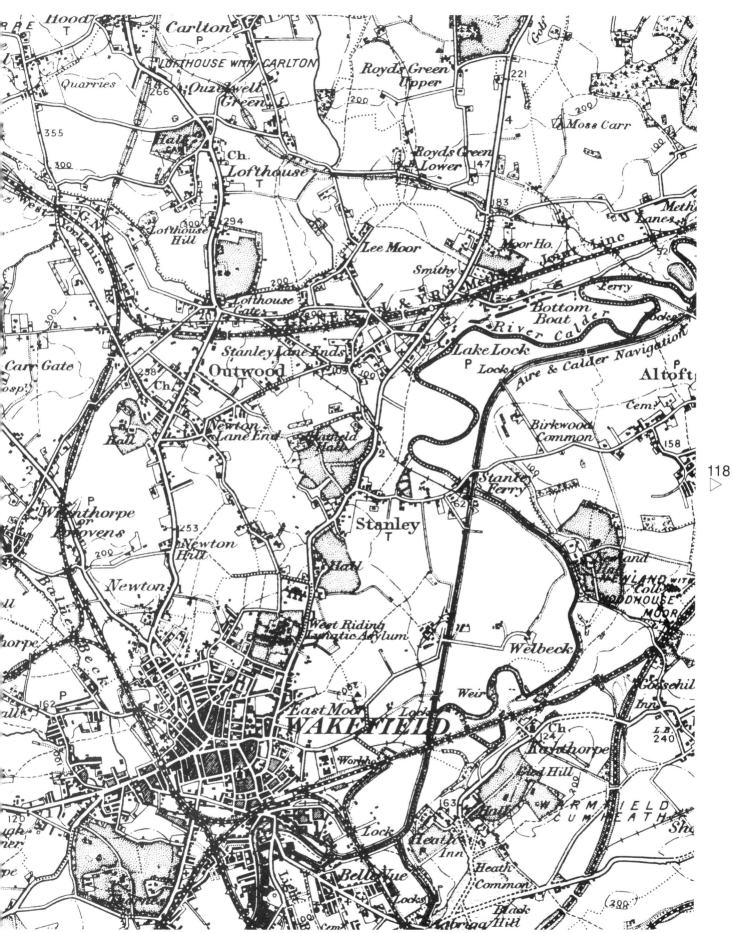

118

Surveyed 1843 - 49 / 1888 - 92. Revised 1908. Published 1911.

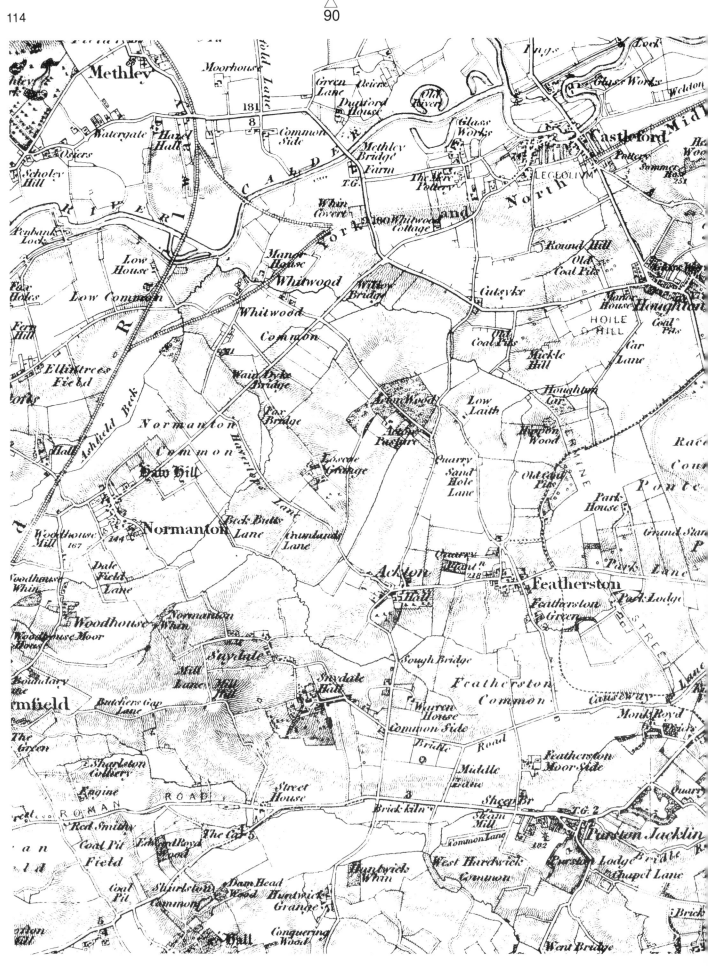

1   2

1 mile approx.

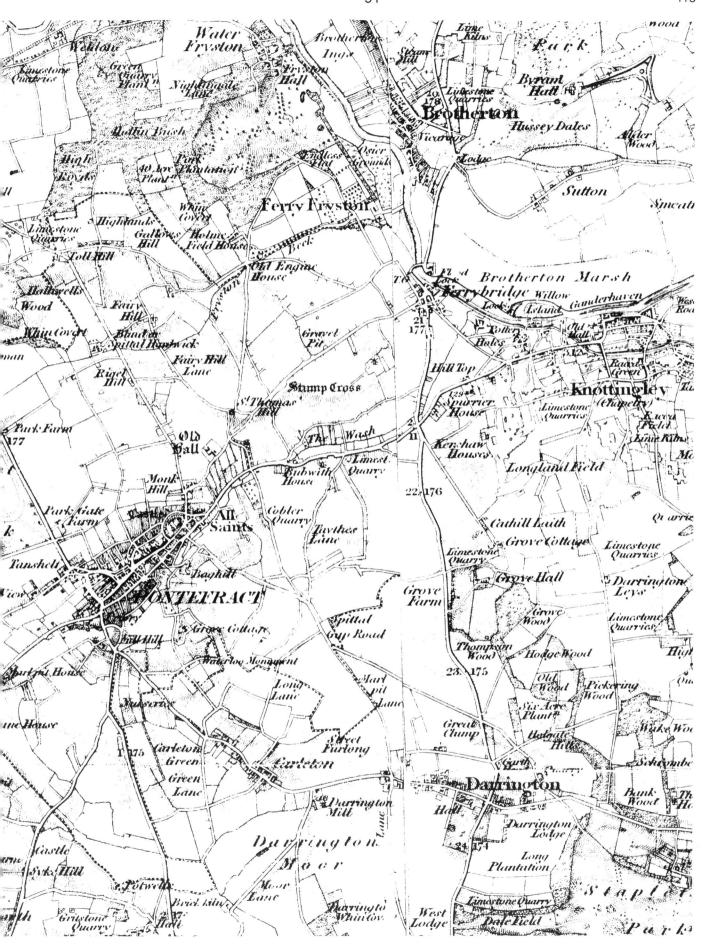

Published 1841.

92

Willow
Grove

Smithy

Smithy

60

Inn

Ch.

METHLEY

Methley
Hall

Inn

59

Scholey
Hill

Inn

Methley
?nes

52

Inn

Flatbank
Lock

Locks

Methley
Junction

STA.

METHLEY
STA.

59

8

RIVER CALDER

38

50

50

STA.

Round
Hill

69

134

Locks

Ferry

Lock

ALTOFTS &
WHITWOOD
STA.

Inn

Ch.

Whitwood

L.B.

100

Inn

100

Inn

100

80

Silkstone
Row

59

Mickle
Hill

Midland Railway

Altofts

Ch.

Smithy

Inn
158

69

Ch.

Hoptown

Ackton
Pasture Wood

M. L. &
Methley Br.

100

Loscoe

Park
Grange

Inn
116

STA.

15

225

Normanton

Smithy

Ch.

100

Smithy

Ch.

Featherstone

111

Woodhouse

Inn

199

100

Ackton
Hall

Inn

209

156

Grange
L.B.

St John's
Terrace

Inn

Snydale

Strawberry
Hill

sehill

Smithy

Warmfield

L.B.
240

200

Fall

115

South Wake
Featherston

L.B.

M.R.

Snydale

Br.

Streethouse

162

STA.

New
Sharlston

Inn

45 Colly

6

Ch.

Smithy
7

ROMAN ROAD

L.B.

SHARLSTON
STA.

Mill

137

Purst

136

Purston Hall

200

Sharlston
Common

L.B.

239

Inn

Huntwick
Grange

1   2

1 mile approx.

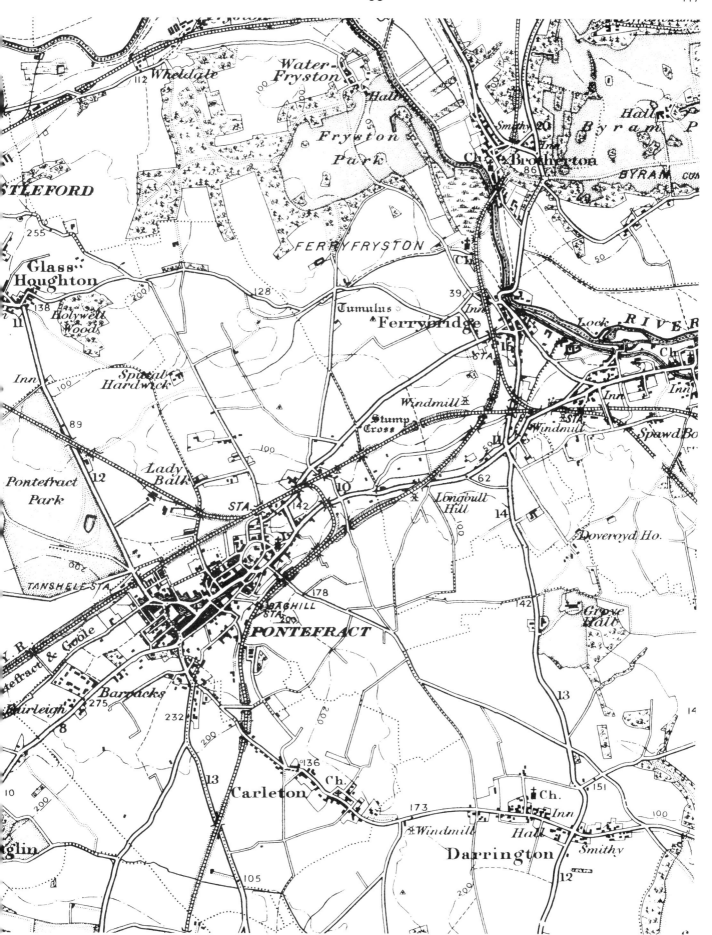

Surveyed 1889 - 92. Revised 1894. Published 1896.

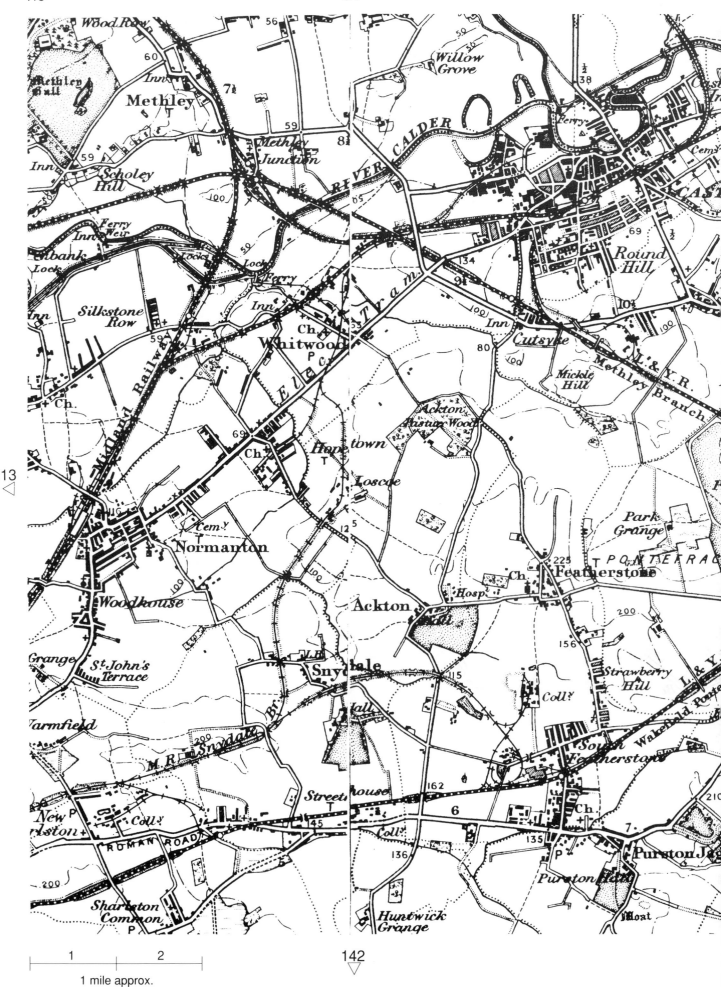

1 mile approx.

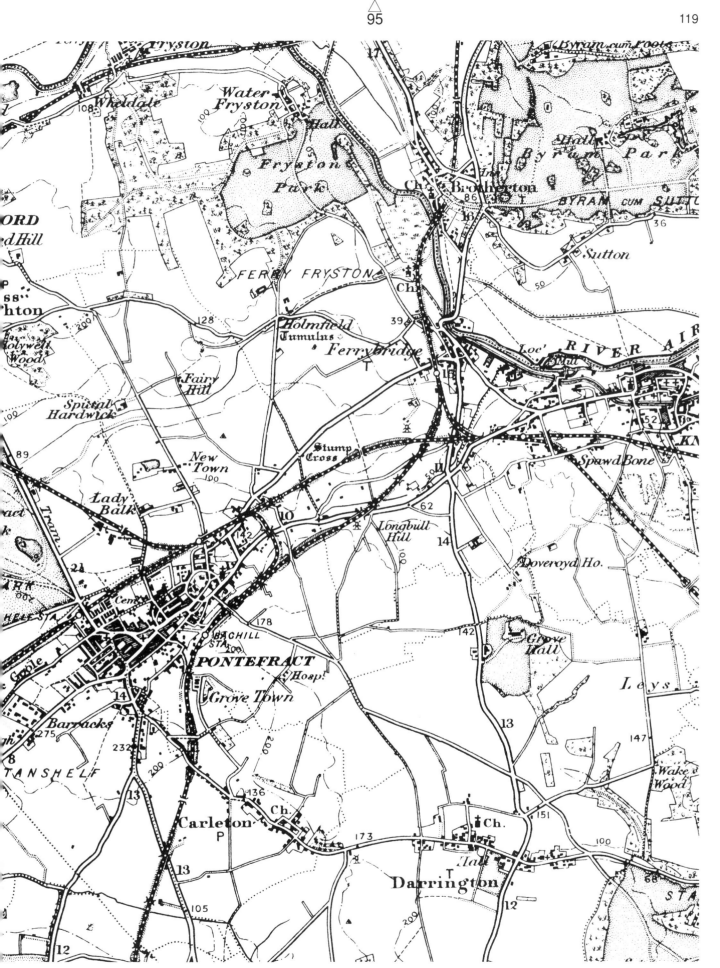

Surveyed 1843 - 49 / 1888 - 92. Revised 1908. Published 1911.

1

2

1 mile approx.

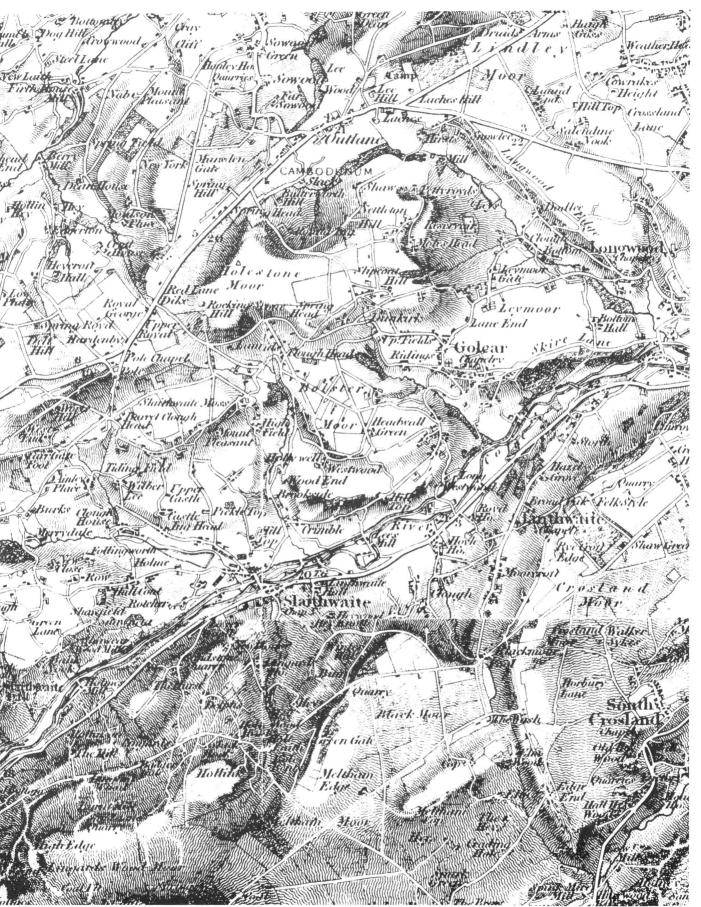

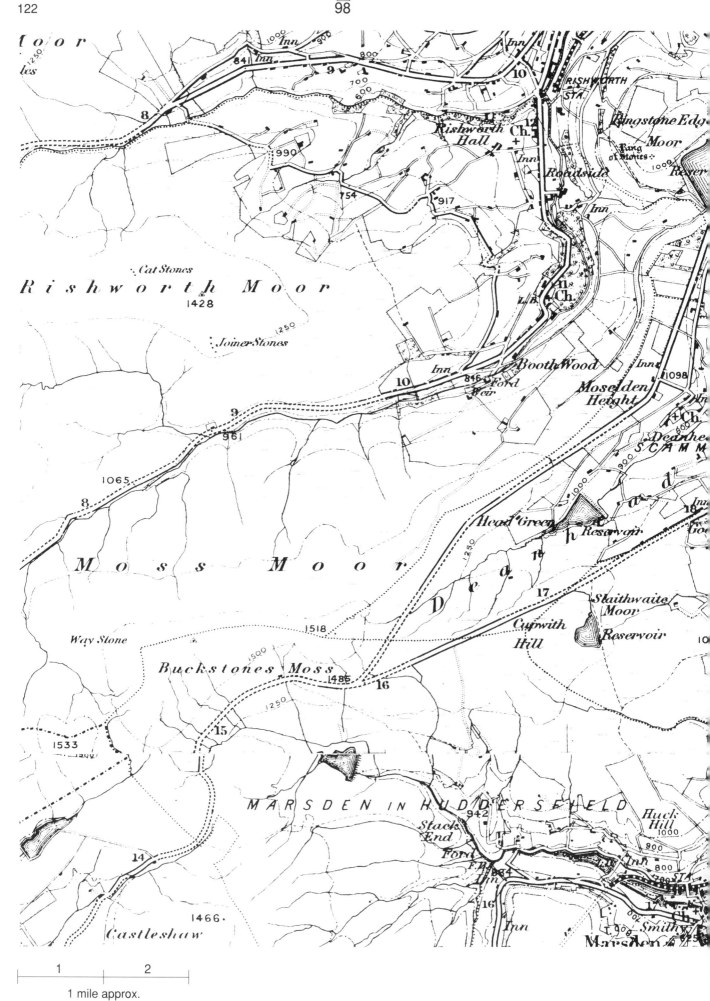

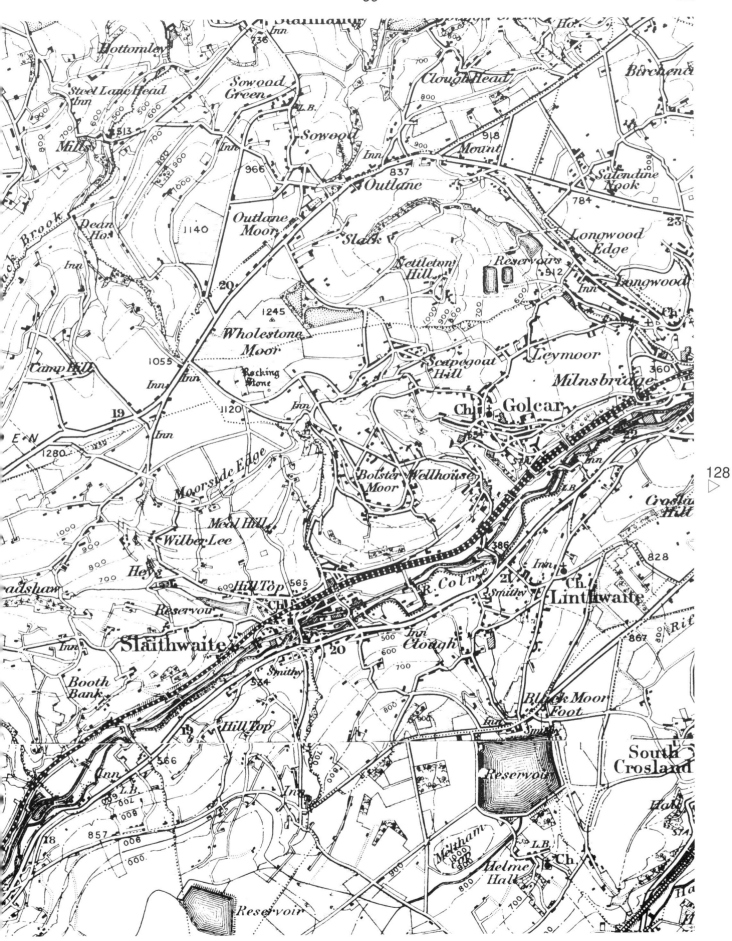

Surveyed 1871 - 72. Revised 1894. Published 1896.

128

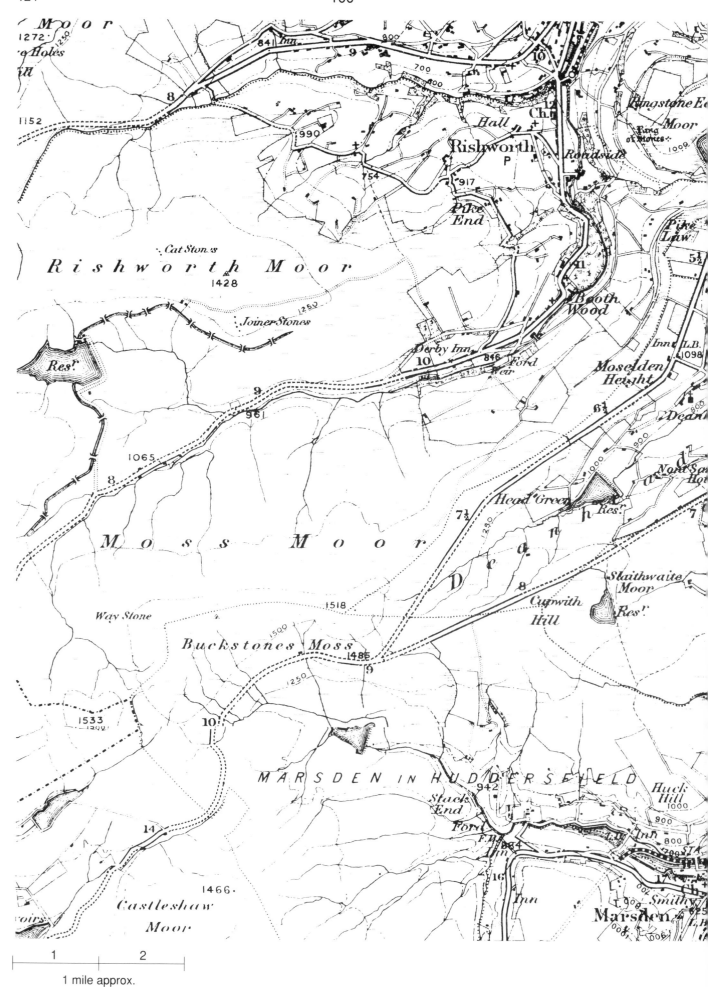

1 mile approx.

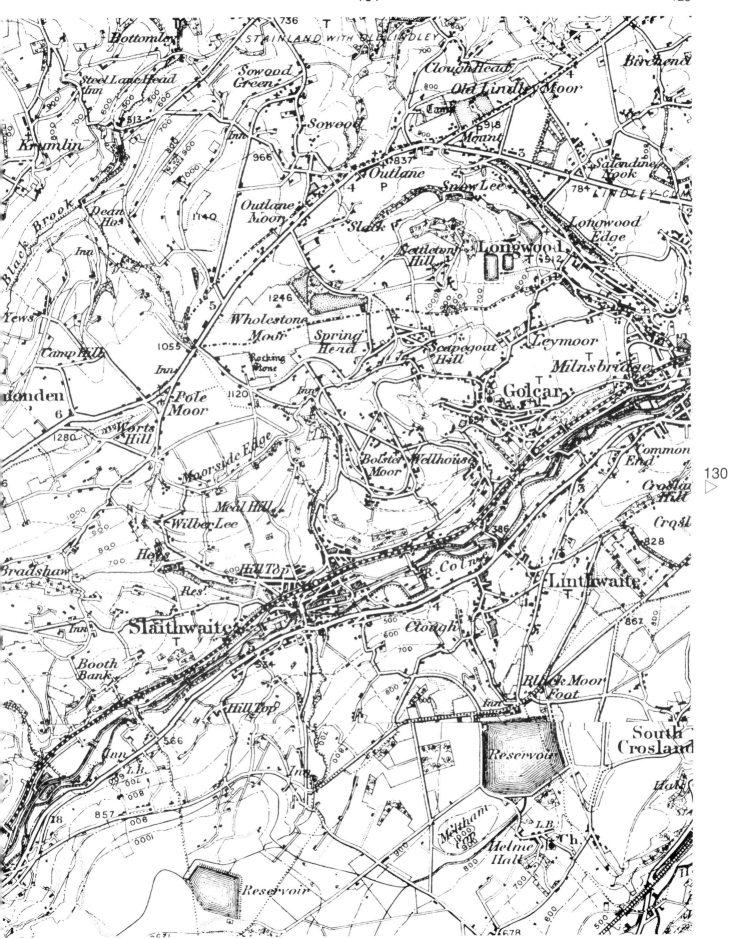

Surveyed 1843 - 49 / 1887 - 93. Published 1911.

1 mile approx.

Published 1841.

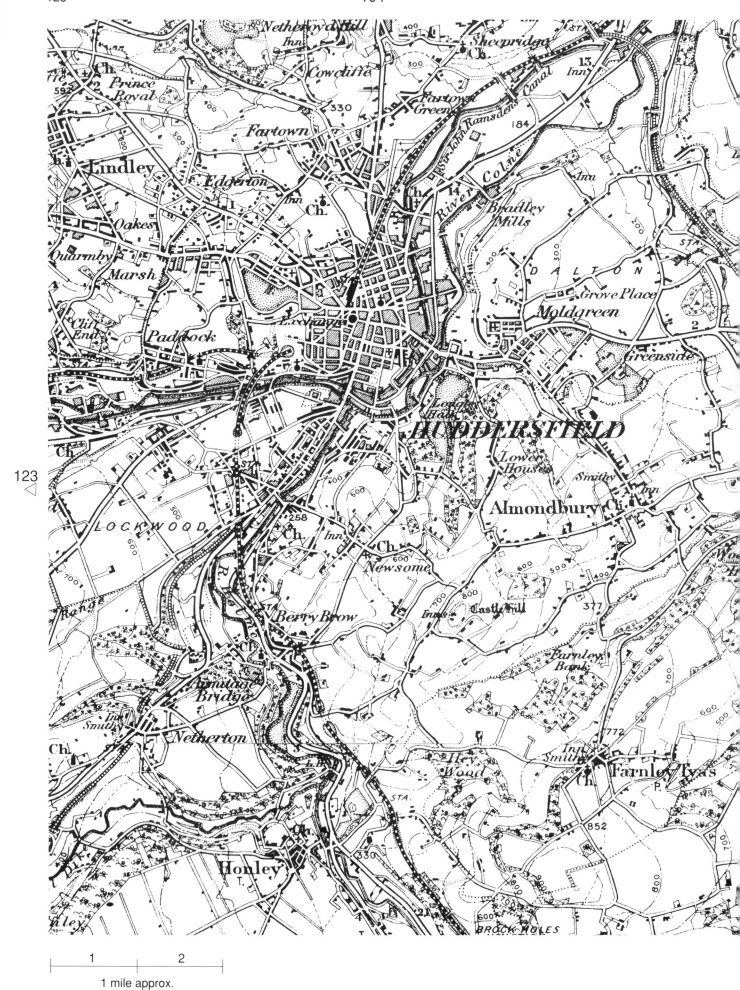

1   2

1 mile approx.

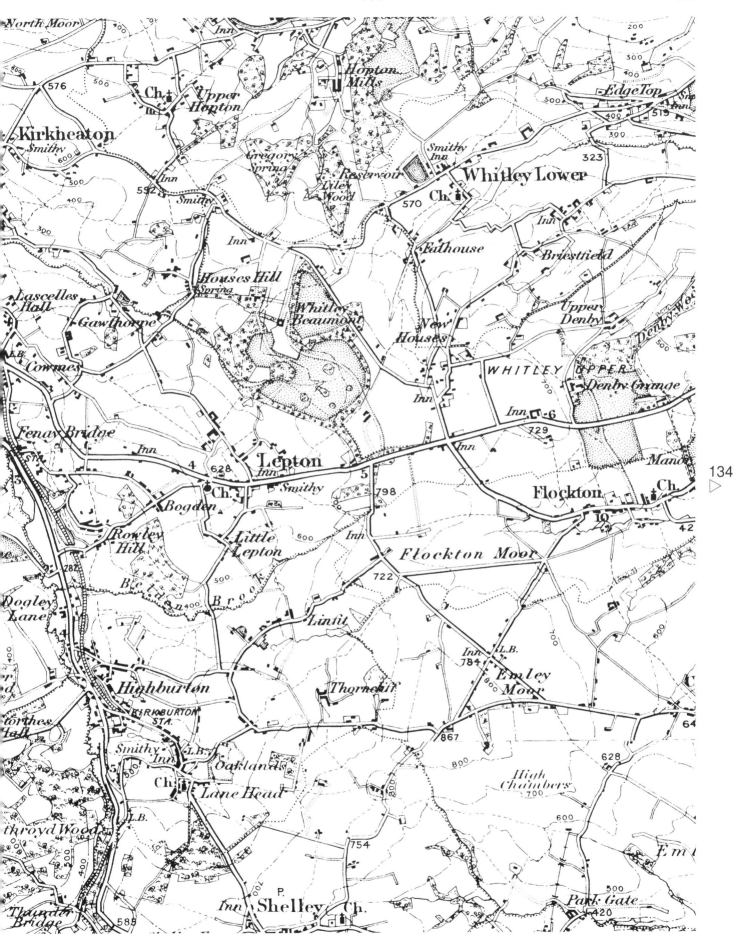

North Moor

Inn

Hopton Mills

Edge Top

Ch.

Upper Hopton

576

500

Kirkheaton

Smithy

600

Gregory Spring

Reservoir

Liley Wood

Smithy Inn

Whitley Lower

323

Inn

500

592

Smithy

570

Ch.

Inn

Fathouse

Briestfield

Inn

Houses Hill

Spring

Whitley Beaumont

New Houses

Upper Denby

Denby Wood

Lascelles Hall

Gawthorpe

WHITLEY UPPER

Denby Grange

Cowmes

Inn

Inn

6

729

Fenay Bridge

Inn

Manor

4

628

Lepton

5

Ch.

134

Flockton

Inn

Smithy

798

Bogden

10

42

Rowley Hill

Little Lepton

600

Inn

Flockton Moor

282

722

Dogley Lane

Belden Brook

400

500

Linfit

Inn 784

L.B.

Emley Moor

Highburton

Thorncliff

KIRKBURTON STA.

forthes Hall

Smithy Inn

L.B.

867

628

Oaklands

High Chambers

700

Ch.

Lane Head

L.B.

600

throyd Wood

400

754

Em

Inn

Shelley

Ch.

Park Gate

420

Thunder Bridge

585

Surveyed 1871 - 72. Revised 1894. Published 1896.

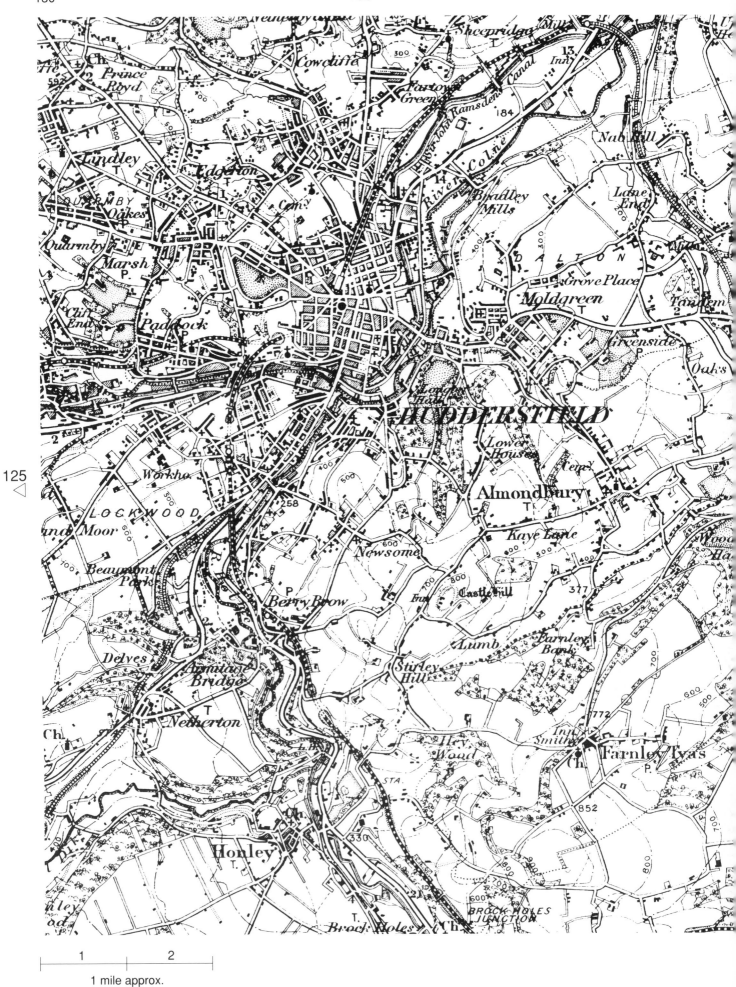

1

2

1 mile approx.

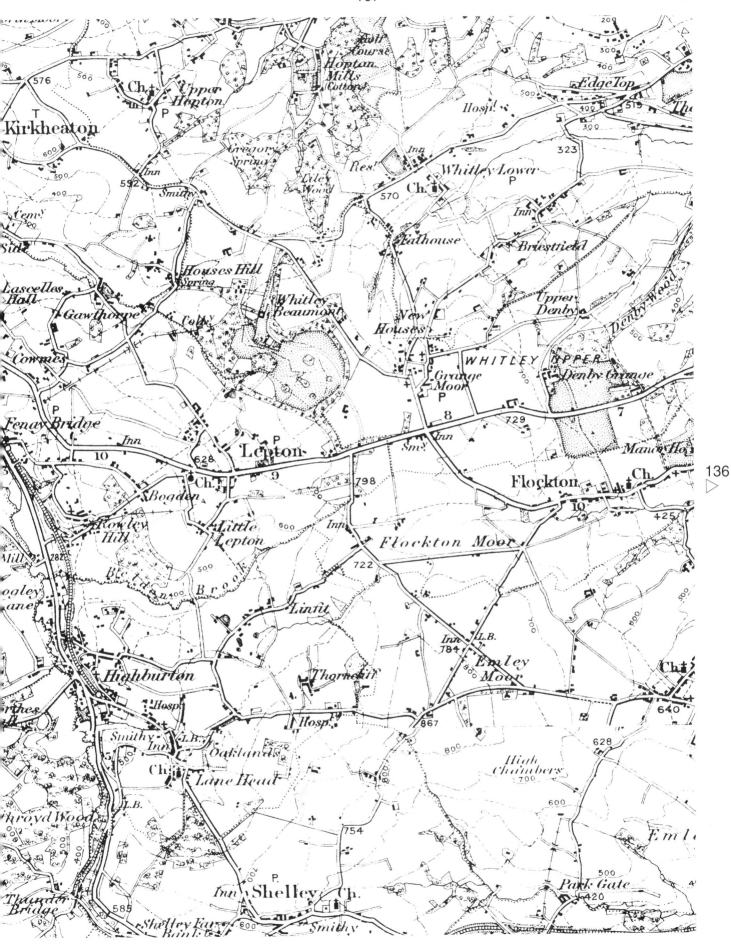

Surveyed 1887 - 93. Revised 1908. Published 1911.

1   2

1 mile approx.

Published 1841.

Smithy

Ch.
Thornhill
Inn

Healey

Locks

Calder & Hebble Navig.

Roda Ho.

Hall
Cliffe

Thornhill Edge

Hostingley Ho.

L.B.

Smithy

Ch.

Smithy Brook

Ch.

200

Inn

Horbu

195

STA.

Ch. Ma

Middlestown

Ch.

Inn

Coxley

Ch.

110

106

Inn

375

Ch.

Netherton

Ford
Inn

8

Inn
Smithy

342

Calder Grove

436

L.P.
Smi

Chapel Hill

S H I T L N C T O N

300

Gre
Cli

4

StonyCliffe
Wood

Bullcliff

568

Newhall

400

**New Hall
Wood**

CRIGGLESTONE
STA.

*Flockton
Green*

321

7

L.B.

9

5

500

Inn

400

Midgley

500

444

*Bank
Wood*

400

500

6

514

West Bretton

405
400

Inn
Smithy

464

*Savin Roya
Wood*

500

Emley

47

Bretton Park

Ch.

300

Hall

L.&YR

500

*Hall
Hill*

400

282

STA.
231
Far

*Emley
Old Hall*

y Park

Lithorop

Long Side

Haigh
Hall

Mill

400

Smithy
8
L.B.
ST.

Clayton Hall

300

Swithen

1	2

1 mile approx.

129

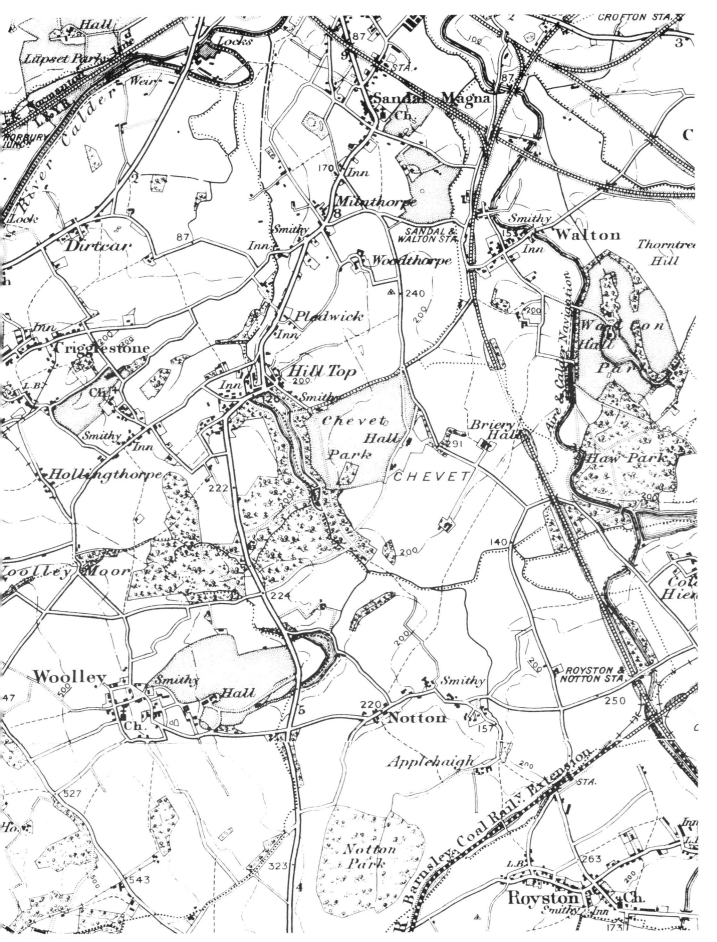

Surveyed 1889 - 92. Revised 1894. Published 1896.

Combs
Thornhill
P
Healey
Rock Ho.
Hall Cliffe
Horbury
T
Ch.
Lancashire
Thornhill Edge
P
Smithy Brook
Ch.
R. Calder
Mill
Calder & Hebble Nav.
Lock
Middlestown
Coxley
Ch.
Calder Grove
P
M. R.
Overton Lo.
Netherton
Inn
Chapel Hill
Golf Course
Stony Cliffe Wood
Great Cliff
HORBURY
New Hall
Bullcliff
CRIGGLESTONE STA.
New Hall Wood
Flockton Green
T
L. B.
Midgley
Inn
West Bretton
P
Kirkby
Bank Wood
Savin Royd Wood
Woolley Edge
Emley
P
Woodhouse Fm.
Bretton Park
Hall
Ch.
L. & Y. R.
Haw Hill
Litherop
Long Side
Mill Sta.
Far Moor Ho.
Emley Old Hall
Cillcar
Haigh
P
Hall
Park
Smithy
L. B. Sta.
Mill
Clayton Hall
Barnsley Br.

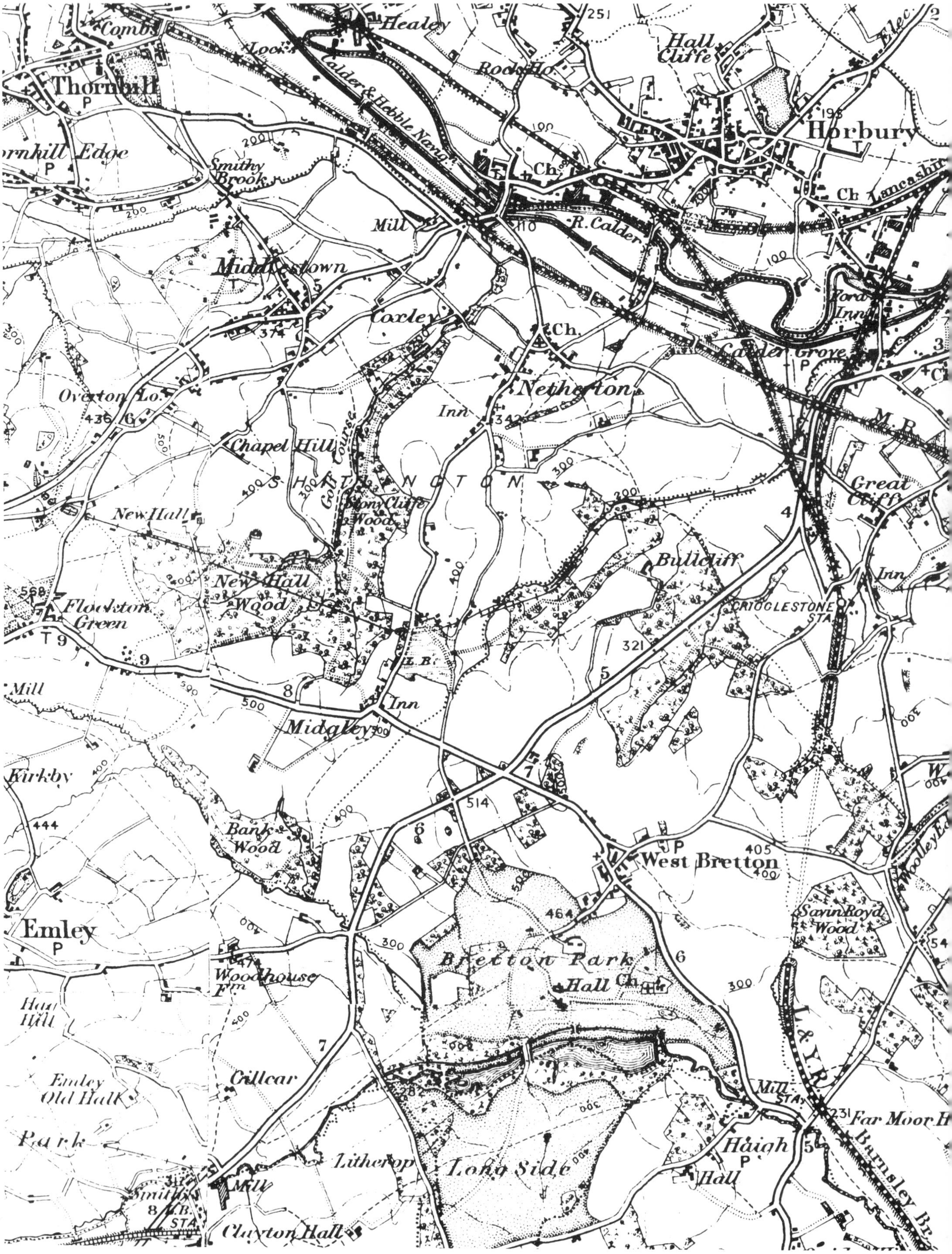

1 mile approx.

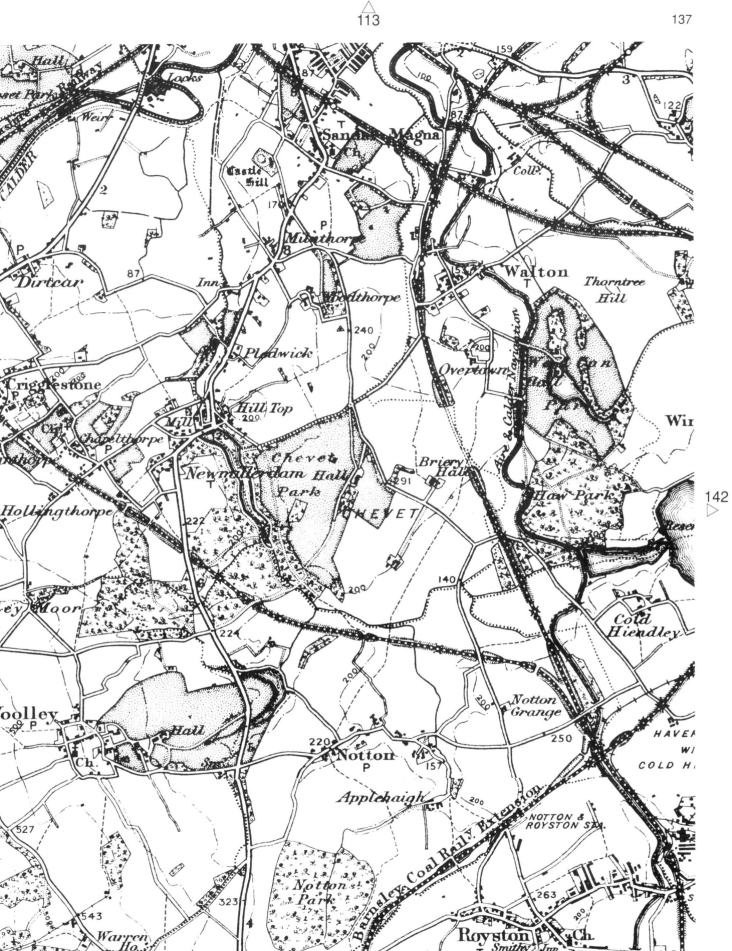

142

Surveyed 1843 - 49 / 1888 - 92. Revised 1908. Published 1911.

1   2

1 mile approx.

Published 1841.

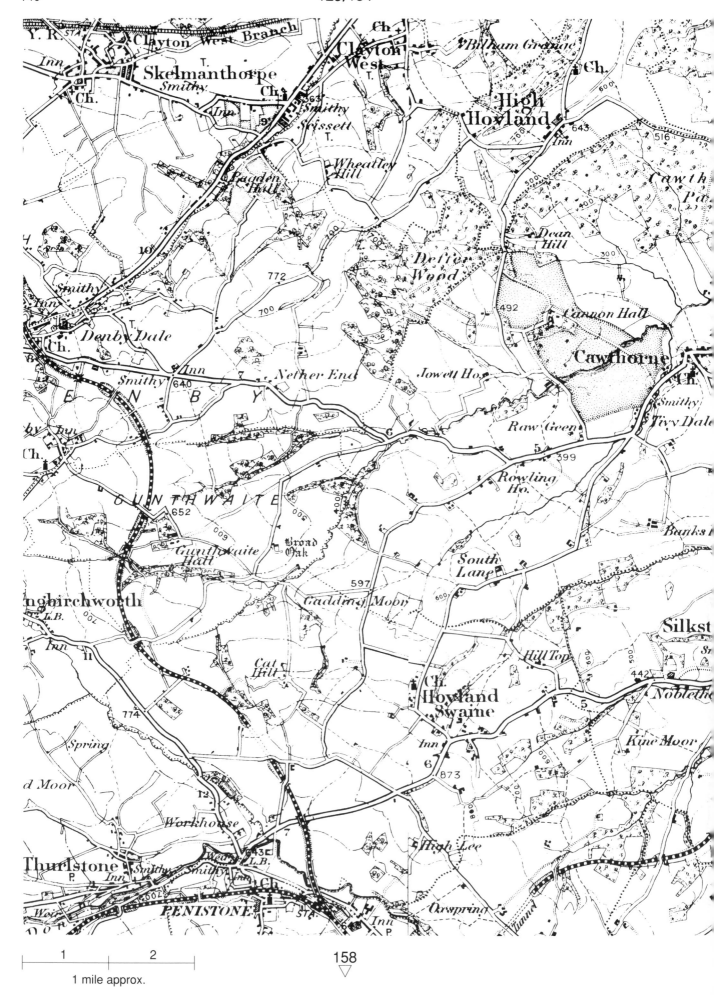

1   2

1 mile approx.

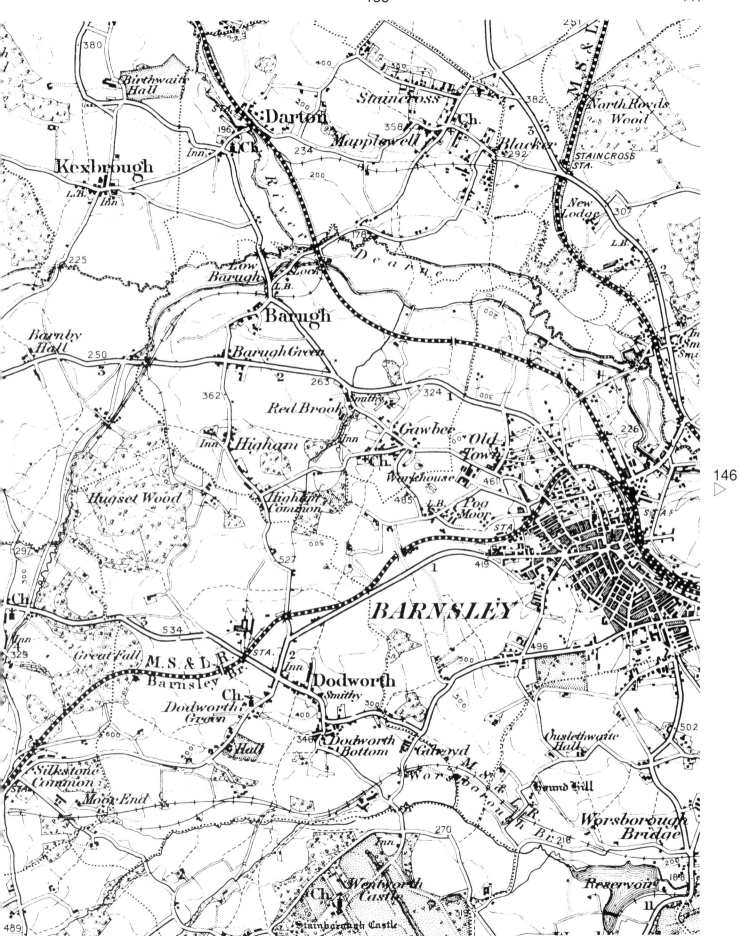

Surveyed 1871 - 72. Revised 1894. Published 1896.

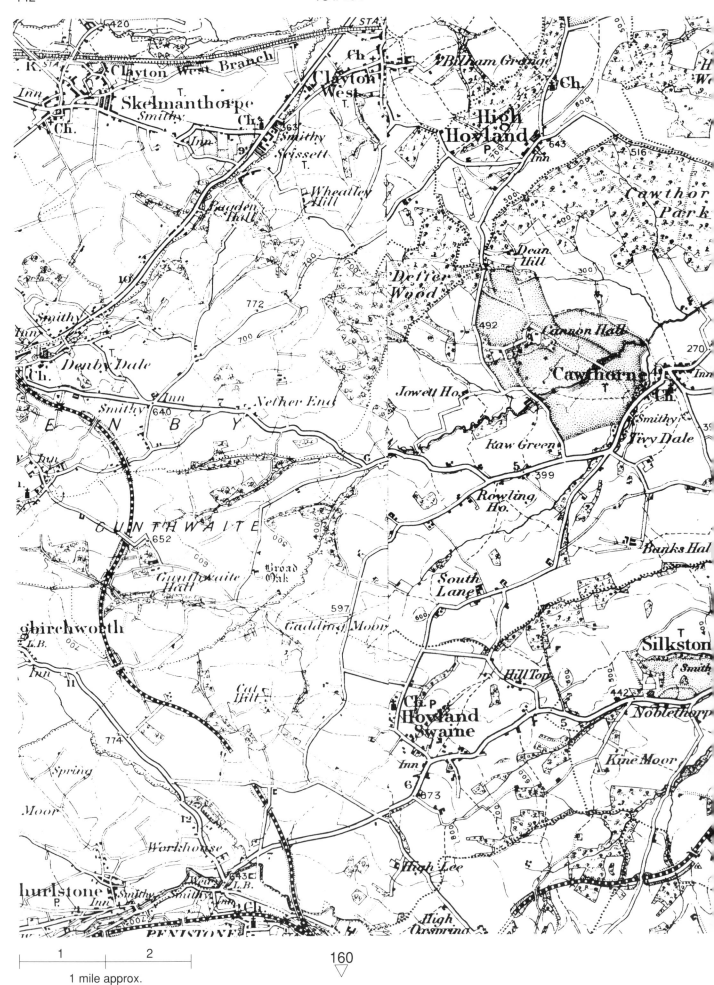

1   2

1 mile approx.

148

1   2

1 mile approx.

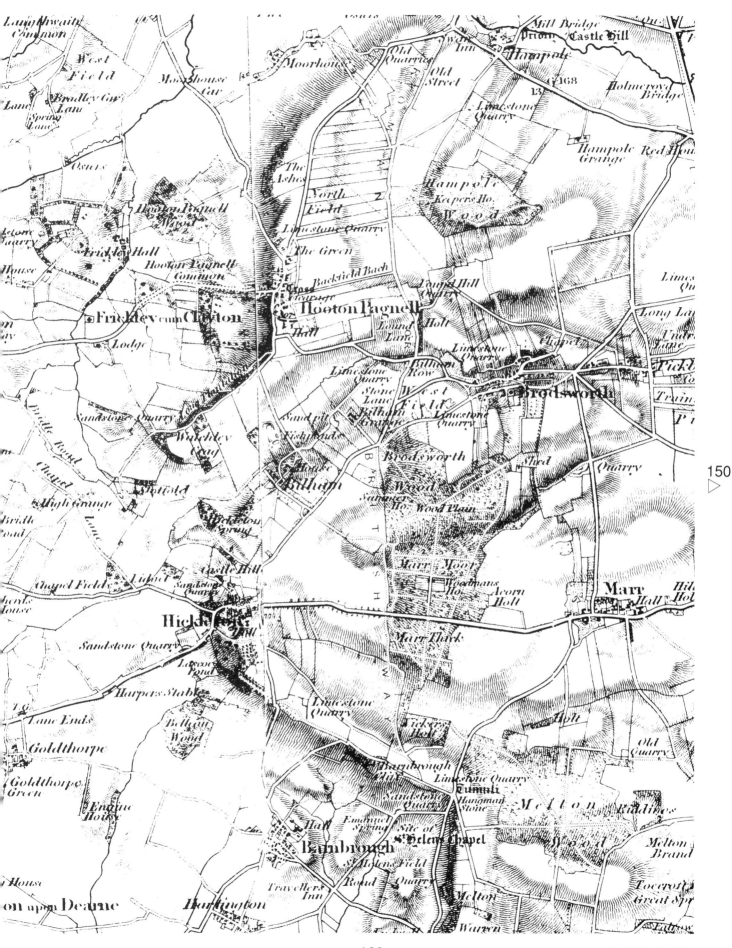

150

Published 1841.

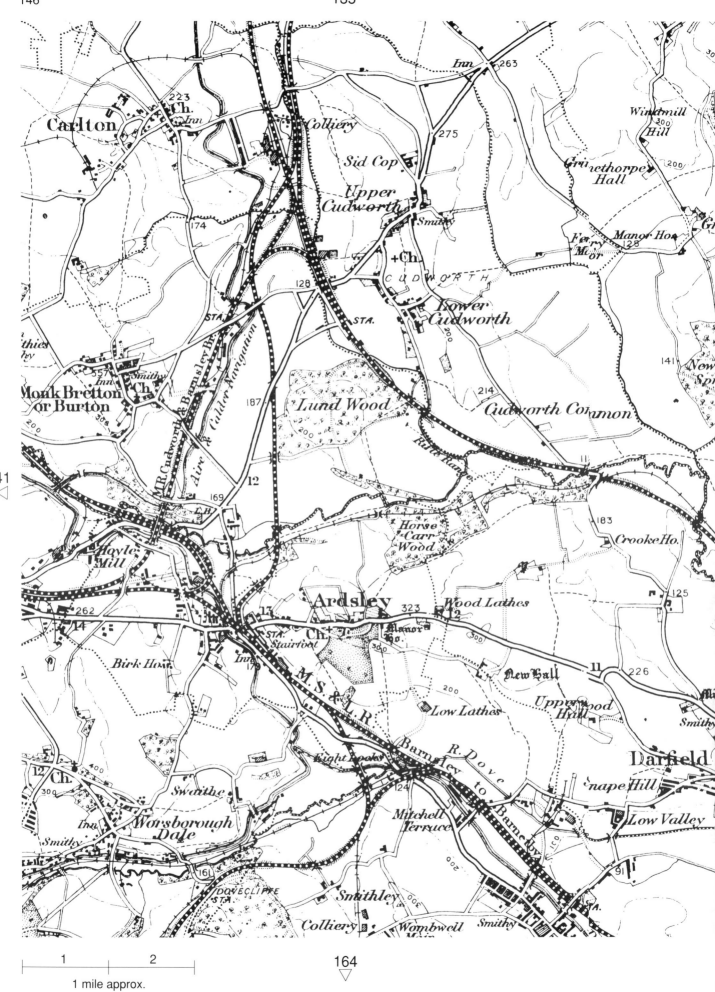

1 mile approx.

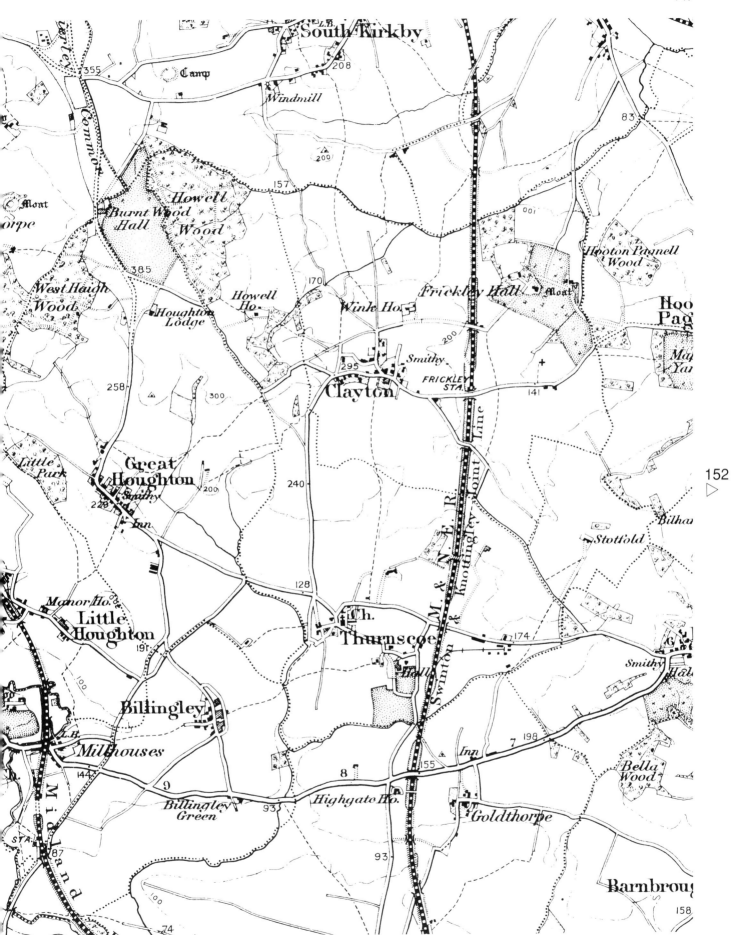

South Kirkby

Camp

355

Windmill

208

200

157

83

Burnt Wood Hall

Howell Wood

C Moat

orpe

West Haugh Wood

170

001

Hooton Pagnell Wood

Howell Ho.

Winte Ho.

Frickley Hall

Moat

Hoo Pag

385

258

300

Houghton Lodge

295

Smithy

FRICKLEY STA.

Clayton

200

141

Little Park

Great Houghton

Smithy

200

240

Ma Ya

229

Inn

Bilha

Stotfold

128

Manor Ho.

Little Houghton

Ch.

Thurnscoe

191

100

Hall

174

Smithy

Hal

Billingley

Millhouses

L.B

144

9

Billingley Green

93

8

155

Inn

7 198

Bella Wood

Highgate Ho.

Goldthorpe

STA

87

100

93

Barnbrou

74

158

Surveyed 1871 - 72. Revised 1894. Published 1896.

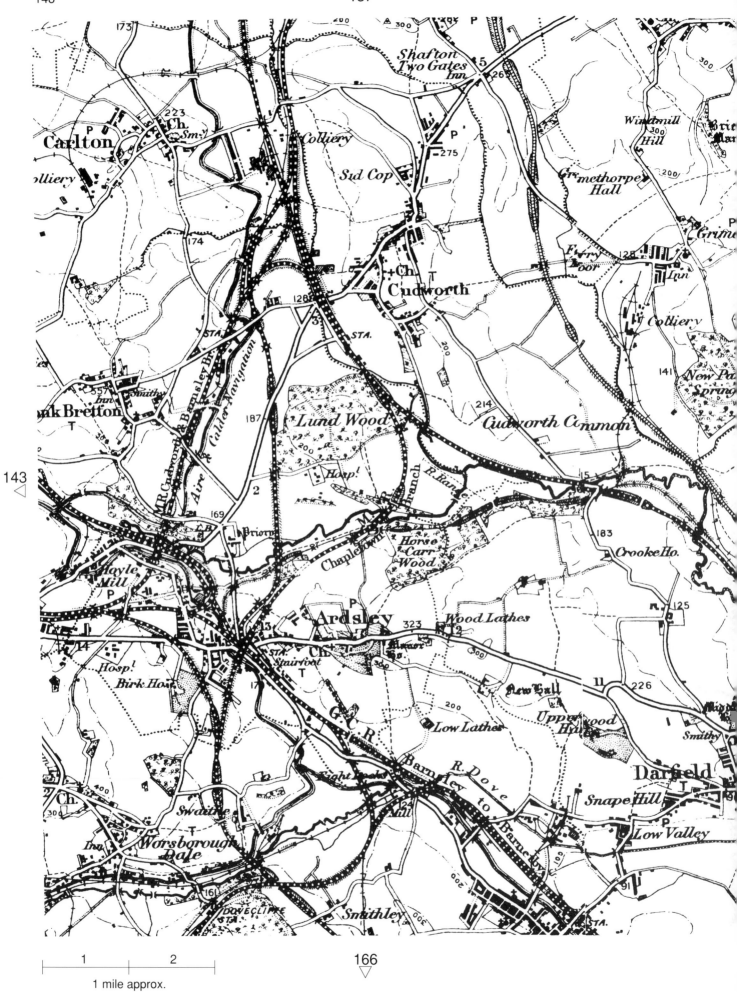

1   2

1 mile approx.

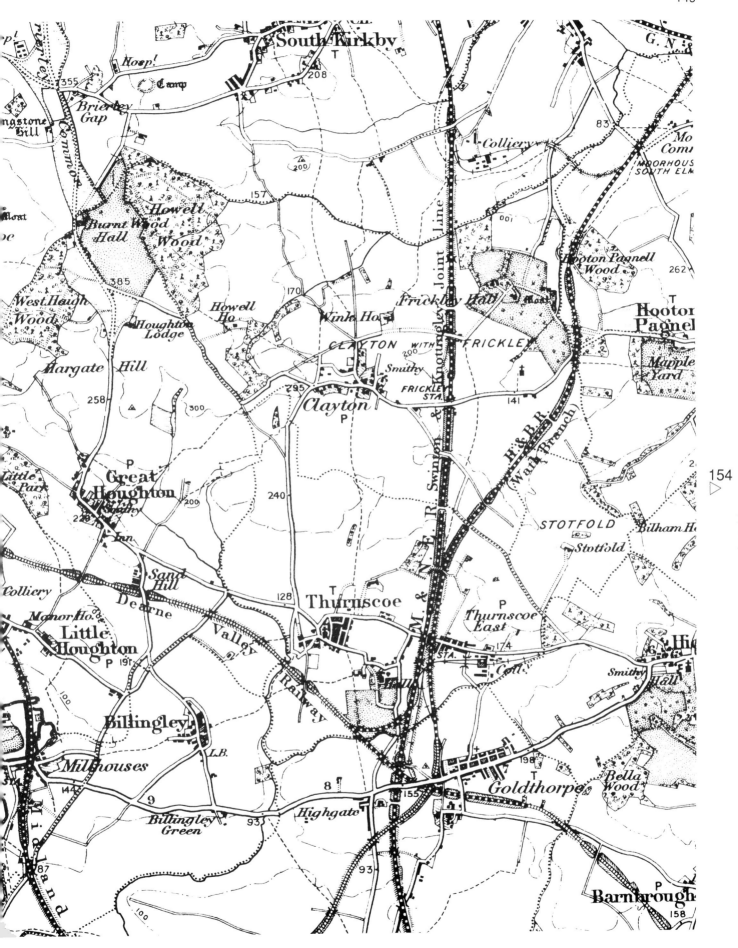

South Kirkby

Hosp!

355

Brierley
Gap

ngstone
Hill

Common

208

Camp

200

157

Colliery

G. N.

83

Mo
Com

MOORHOUSE
SOUTH ELM

Howell
Wood

Burnt Wood
Hall

385

Hooton Pagnell
Wood

262

West Haugh
Wood

Moat

170

Howell
Ho

Wink Ho

Frickley Hall

Hooton
Pagnel

T

Hargate Hill

Houghton
Lodge

CLAYTON WITH
200

Smithy

FRICKLEY

Mapple
Yard

258

295

Clayton

FRICKLEY
STA.

141

H. & B. R.
(Wath Branch)

300

P

240

M. & N. E. R. Swinton & Knottingley Joint Line

STOTFOLD

Bilham Ho

154

Little
Park

Great
Houghton

Smithy

200

Stotfold
Stotfold

Inn

Colliery

Sand
Hill

Dearne

128

Thurnscoe

T

P

Thurnscoe
East

Manor Ho.

Little
Houghton

Valley

STA.

174

Coll.

Smithy

Hall

P

191

Railway

Billingley

Beam

198

Bella
Wood

Millhouses

L.B.

144

9

8

155

Goldthorpe

T

Billingley
Green

93

Highgate

Midland

187

100

93

P

Barnbrough

158

Surveyed 1843 - 49 / 1888 - 92. Revised 1908. Published 1911.

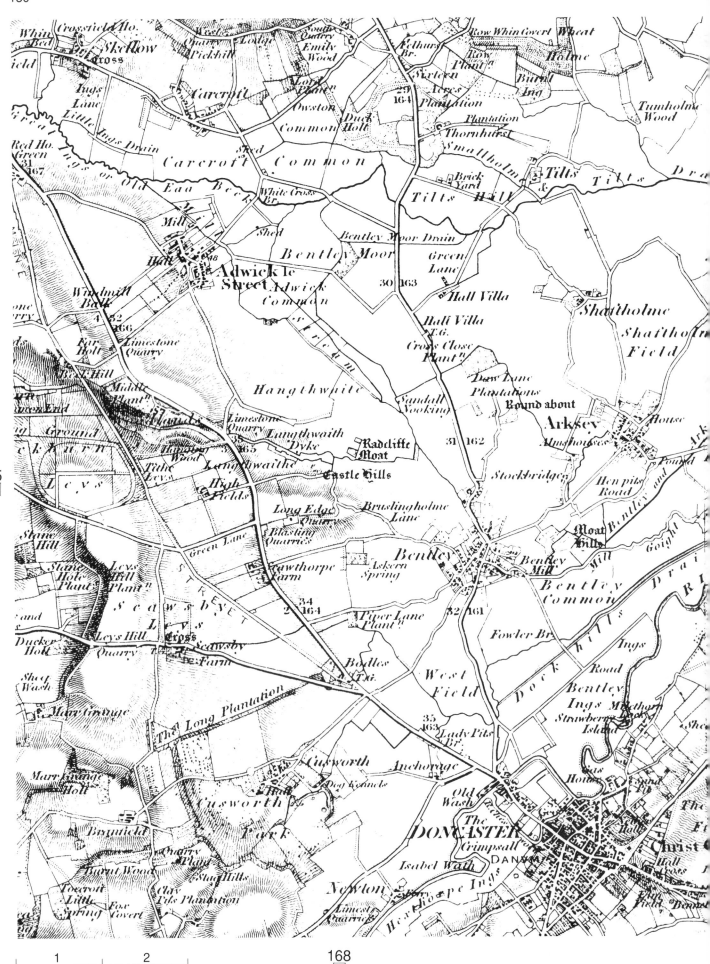

1   2

1 mile approx.

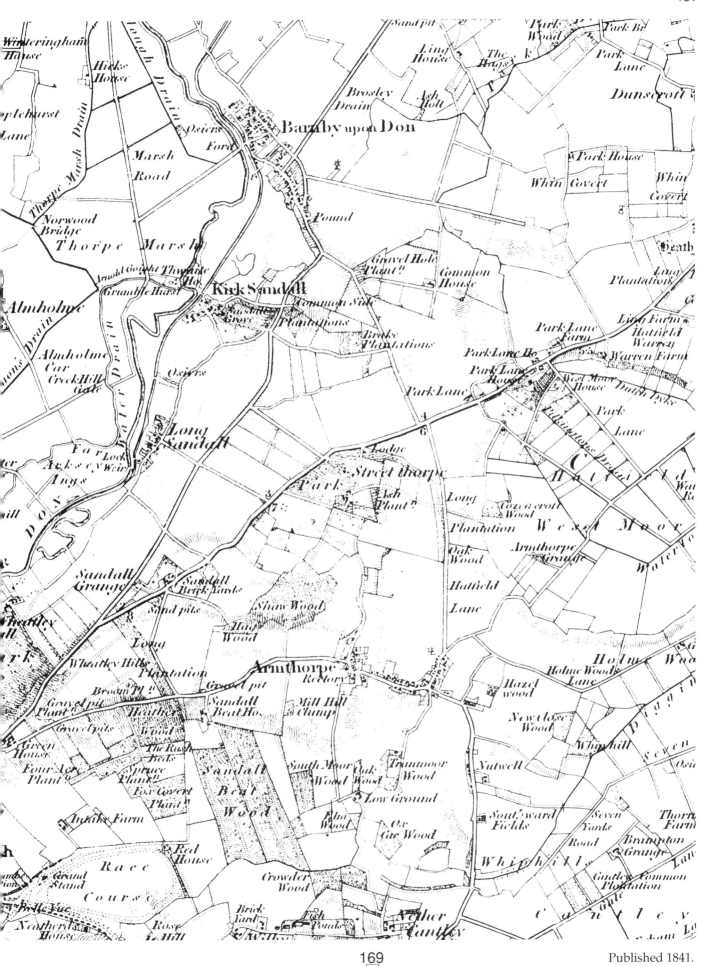

Published 1841.

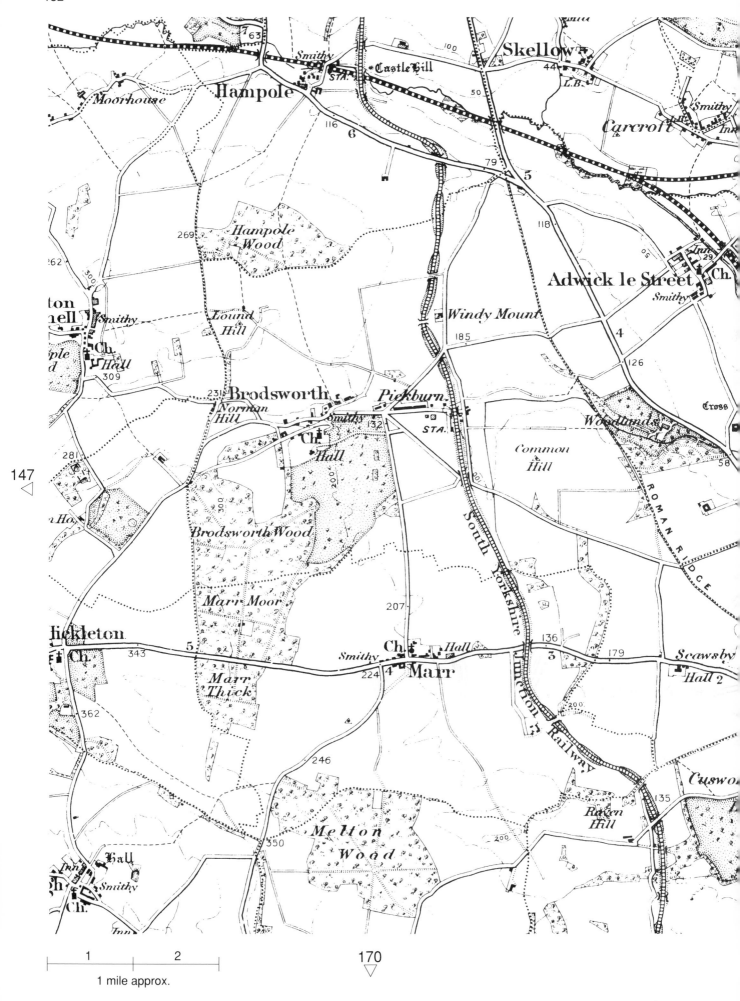

Moorhouse

Smithy

763

Castle Hill

Skellow

44

100

50

L.B.

Carcroft

Smithy

Inn

Hampole

116

6

79

5

118

269

Hampole Wood

95

Inn

29

Ch.

Adwick le Street

Smithy

262

300

Windy Mount

4

126

ton nell

Smithy

Lound Hill

185

ple d

Ch.

Hall

309

Brodsworth

231

Piekburn

Common Hill

Woodlands

Cross

58

Norman Hill

Smithy

132

STA.

281

Ch.

Hall

200

147

Brodsworth Wood

300

207

ROMAN RIDGE

n Ho

South Yorkshire

136

179

Scawsby

Hall 2

Marr Moor

Hickleton

Ch.

343

5

Smithy

Ch.

Hall

Marr

3

362

Marr Thick

224

4

200

Junction

Railway

Cuswo

246

135

Raven Hill

350

Melton

200

Inn

Hall

Wood

 h

Smithy

Ch.

Inn

1   2

1 mile approx.

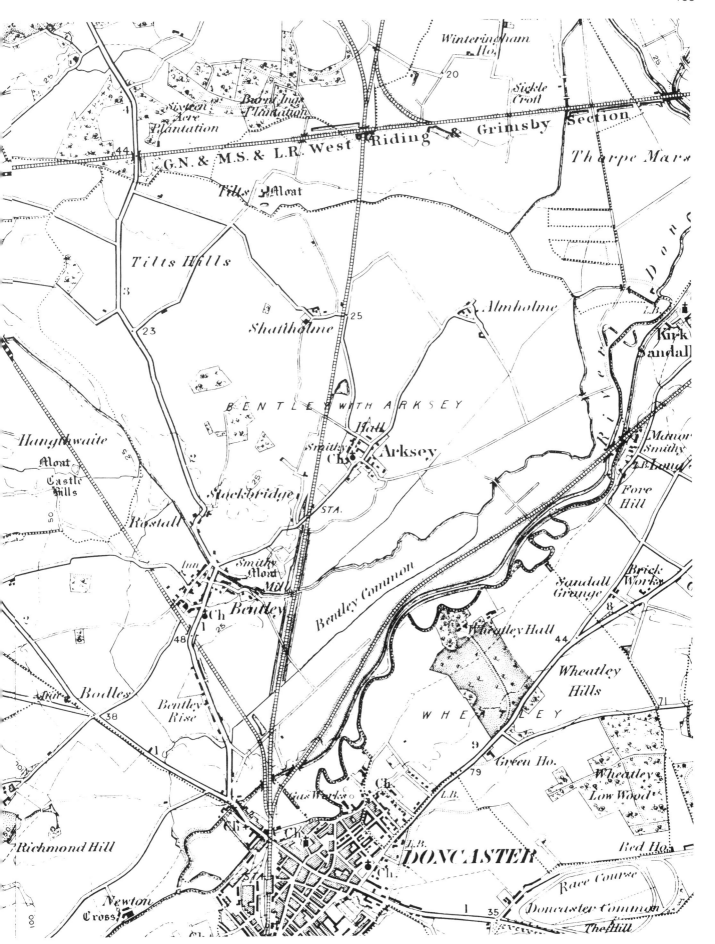

Winteringham Ho.

Sickle Croft

G.N. & M.S. & L.R. West Riding & Grimsby Section

Thorpe Marsh

Sixteen Acre Plantation

Brant Ing Plantation

Tilts Moat

Tilts Hills

Shaftholme

Almholme

Kirk Sandall

BENTLEY WITH ARKSEY

Hall

Arksey

Ch.

Smithy

Manor

Smithy

Fore Hill

Hangthwaite

Moat

Castle Hills

Stockbridge

STA.

Restall

Inn

Smithy Moat

Mill

Bentley Common

Sandall Grange

Brick Works

Ch. Bentley

Wheatley Hall

Bodles

Bentley Rise

Wheatley Hills

WHEATLEY

Green Ho.

Wheatley Low Wood

Richmond Hill

Gas Works

Ch.

L.B.

DONCASTER

Ch.

Red Ho.

Newton Cross

Race Course

Doncaster Common

The Hill

Surveyed 1871 - 72 / 1884 - 91. Revised 1894. Published 1895 - 96.

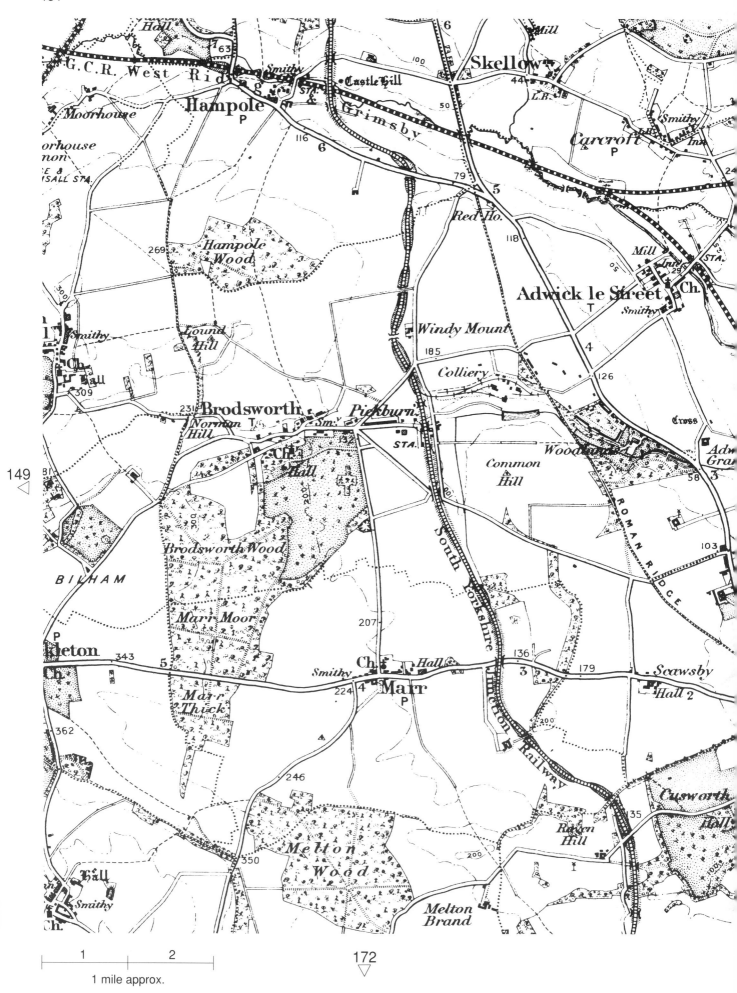

149

1 mile approx.

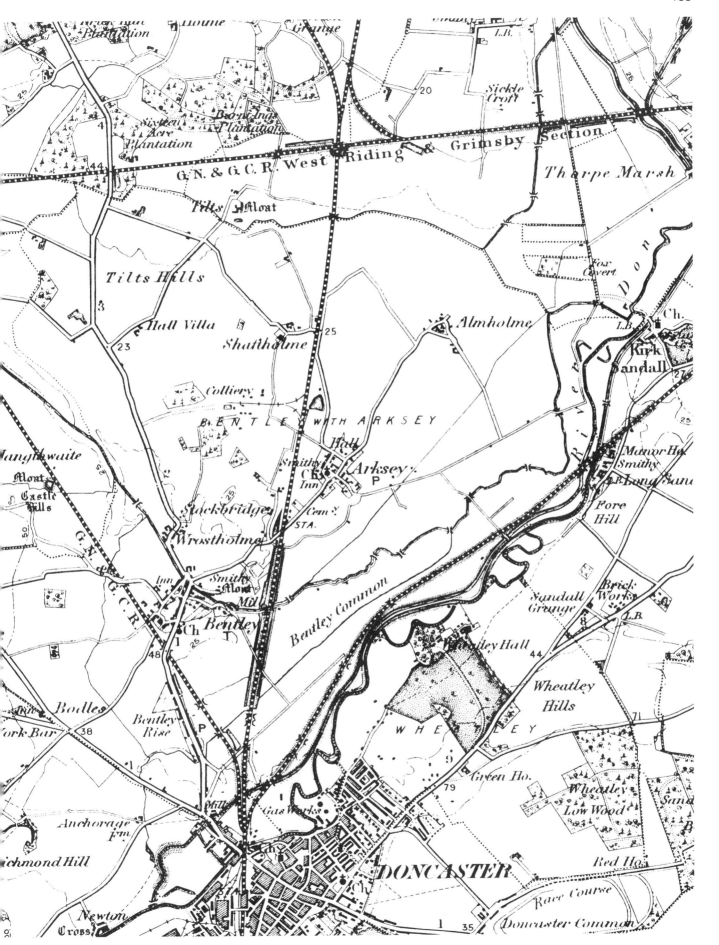

173 Surveyed 1843 - 49 / 1884 - 91. Revised 1905 - 1908. Published 1907 - 11.

1 mile approx.

Published 1841.

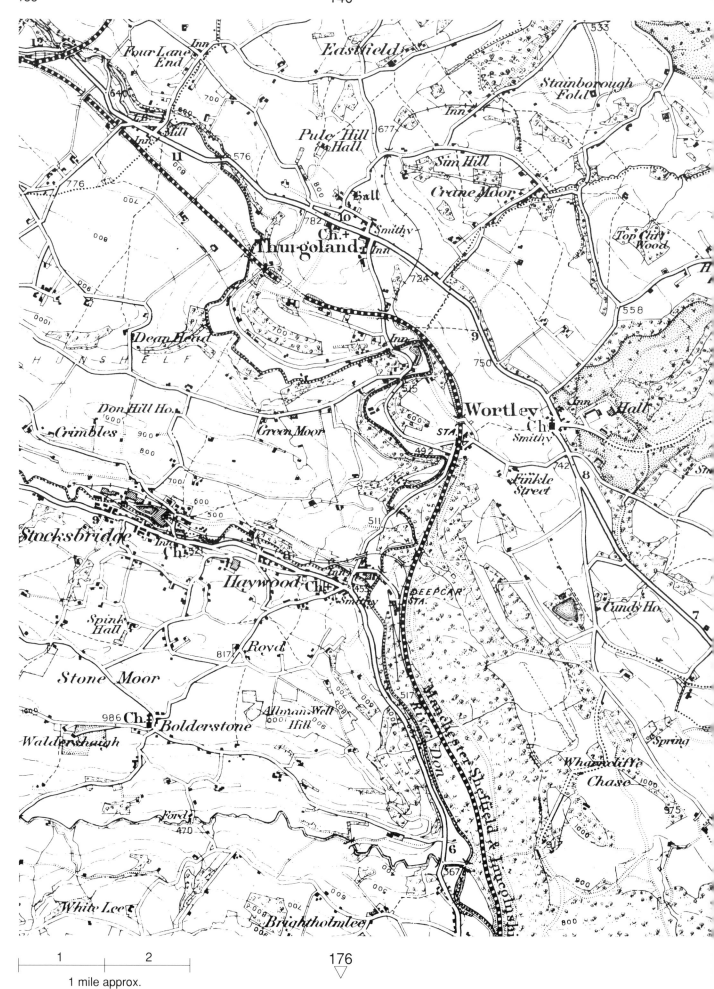

1 mile approx.

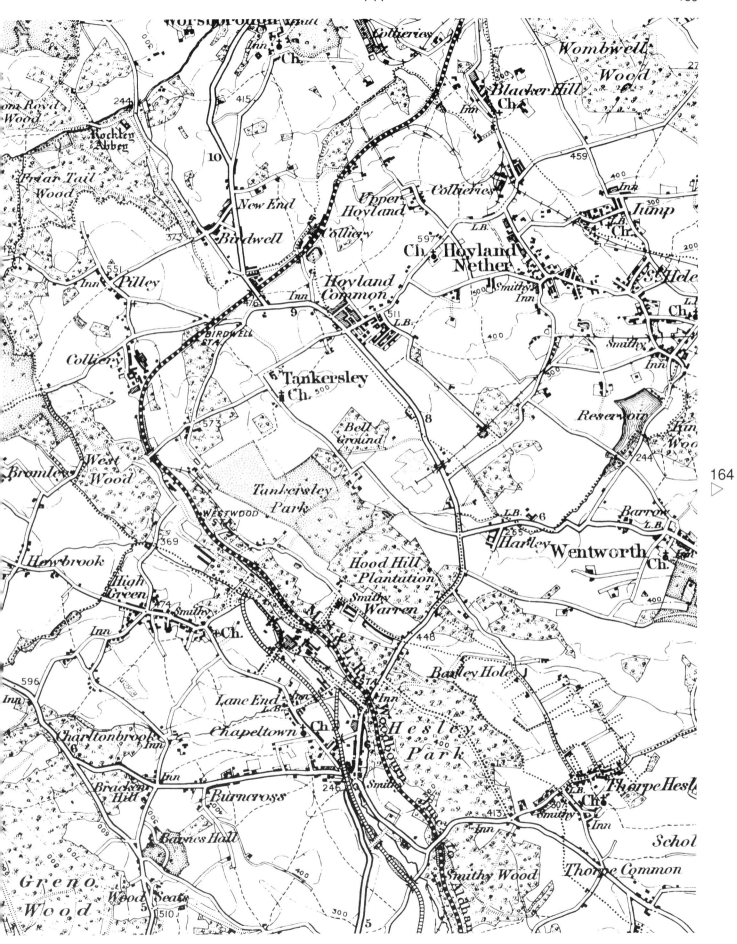

Surveyed 1871 - 72. Revised 1894. Published 1896.

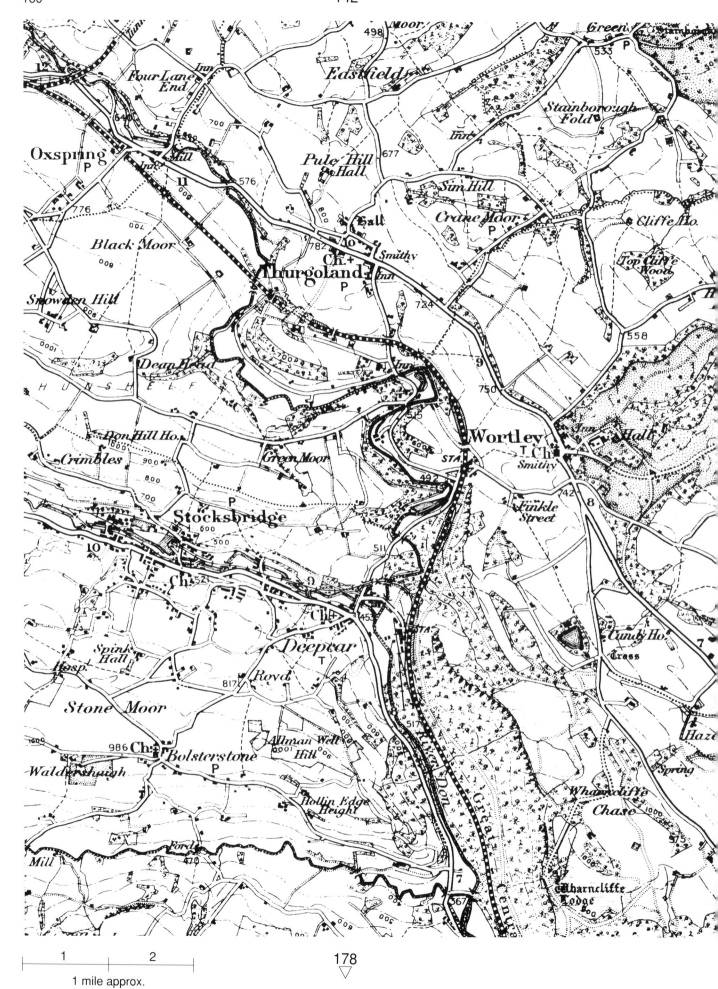

1   2

1 mile approx.

Worsbrough Hall

Colliery

Wombwell Wood

Blacker Hill

Platts Common

Upper Hoyland

Collieries

Jump

Birdwell

Ch.

Colliery

Ch. Hoyland Nether

Hoyland Common

Pilley

Inn

Colliery

Moat

Tankersley
Ch.

Bell
Ground

M.R.

Reservoir

King Wood

Branch

West Wood

Bromley

Tankersley
Park

Westwood

Barrow

Harley

Wentworth

Howbrook

Hood Hill
Plantation

Hood
Hill

Ch.

High Green

Smithy Warren

Near Potter
Hill

Barley Hole

Lane End

Inn

Hesley
Park

Charltonbrook

Chapeltown

Bracken Hill

Burncross

Thorpe Hesle

Raines Hall

Greno
Wood Seats

Smithy Wood

Thorpe Common

Schole

179 Surveyed 1843 - 49 / 1884 - 91. Revised 1905 - 1908. Published 1907 - 11.

1   2

1 mile approx.

Published 1841.

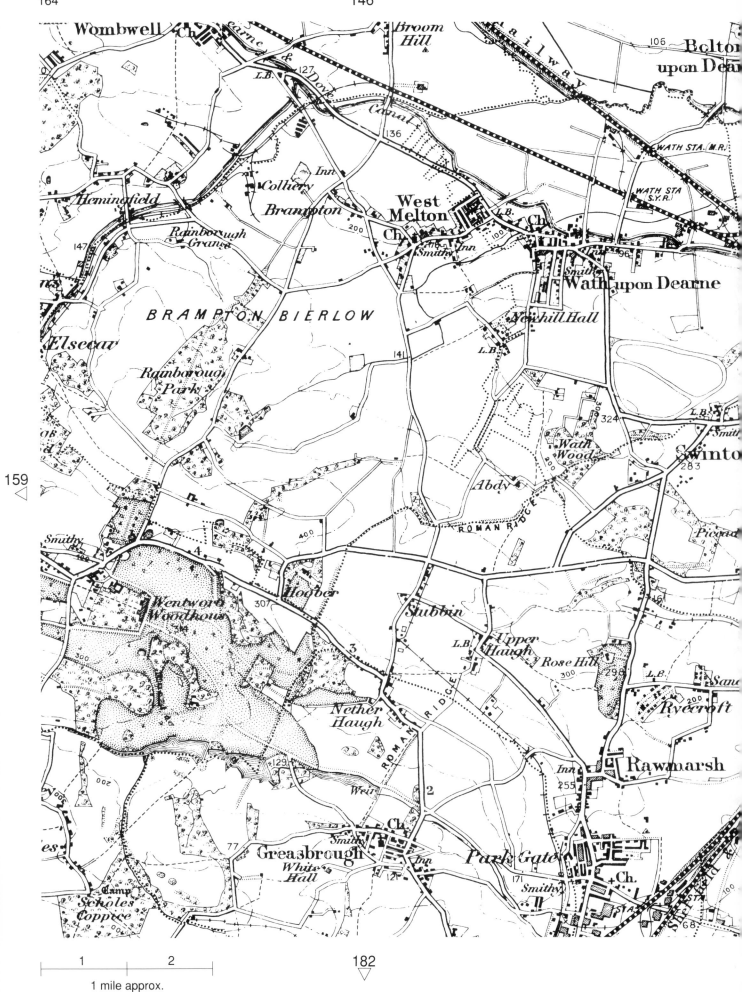

Wombwell Ch.

Broom
Hill

Railway

106 Bolton
upon Dear

L.B.
127

Canal

136

WATH STA. M.R.

Inn

Colliery

Brampton

WATH STA
S.Y.R.

West
Melton
Ch.

Hemingfield

Rainborough
Grange

200

L.B.

100

Smithy Inn

Ch.

Smithy

Wath upon Dearne

147

BRAMPTON BIERLOW

Newhill Hall

Elsecar

141

L.B.

324

Wath
Wood

Swinton

Rainborough
Park

283

Abdy

200

Picga

400

ROMAN RIDGE

Smithy

4

Hoober

Stubbin

R

Wentworth
Woodhouse

307

L.B.

Upper
Haugh

Rose Hill

300

298

L.B.

San

300

3

ROMAN RIDGE

Ryecroft

Nether
Haugh

129

Weir

2

Inn

255

Rawmarsh

Ch.

Smithy

77

Greasbrough

White
Hall

Inn

Park Gate

Ch.

Smithy

Camp
Scholes
Coppice

68

1   2

1 mile approx.

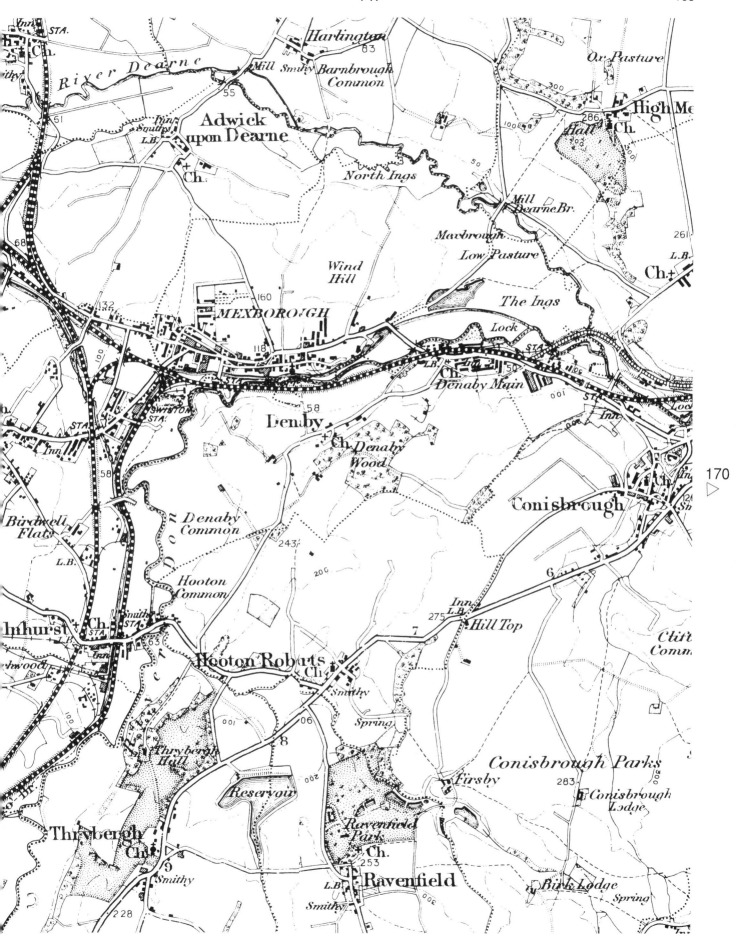

Surveyed 1871 - 72. Revised 1894. Published 1896.

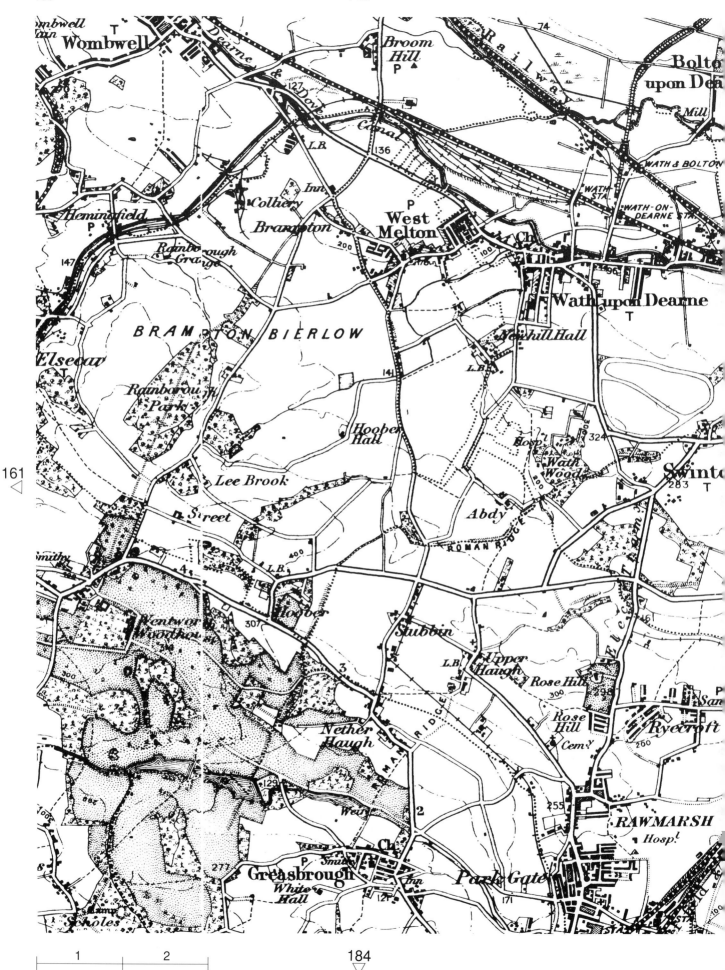

Wombwell

Dearne

Broom
Hill
P

Railwa

Bolto
upon Dea

Mill

127

WATH & BOLTON

Colliery

136

Inn

WATH
STA

WATH-ON-
DEARNE STA

Hemingfield
P

Brampton

West
Melton

P

Ch

147

Rainborough
Grange

200

100

Wath upon Dearne
T

BRAMPTON BIERLOW

Newhill Hall

L.B

Elsecar
T

Rainborough
Park

141

Hooper
Hall

Hosp!

324

Wath
Wood

Swinto
283
T

Lee Brook

Abdy

ROMAN RIDGE

Street

400

L.B

Hooper

307

Stubbin

L.B

Upper
Haugh

Rose Hill
300

298

Smithy

3

Nether
Haugh

Rose
Hill
Cem!

Ryecroft
260

Sa

Wentworth
Woodhouse

300

MAIN RIDGE

255

RAWMARSH

2

Hosp!

Weir

Ch

277

Greasbrough

Inn

Park Gate

171

White
Hall

Scholes

1   2

1 mile approx.

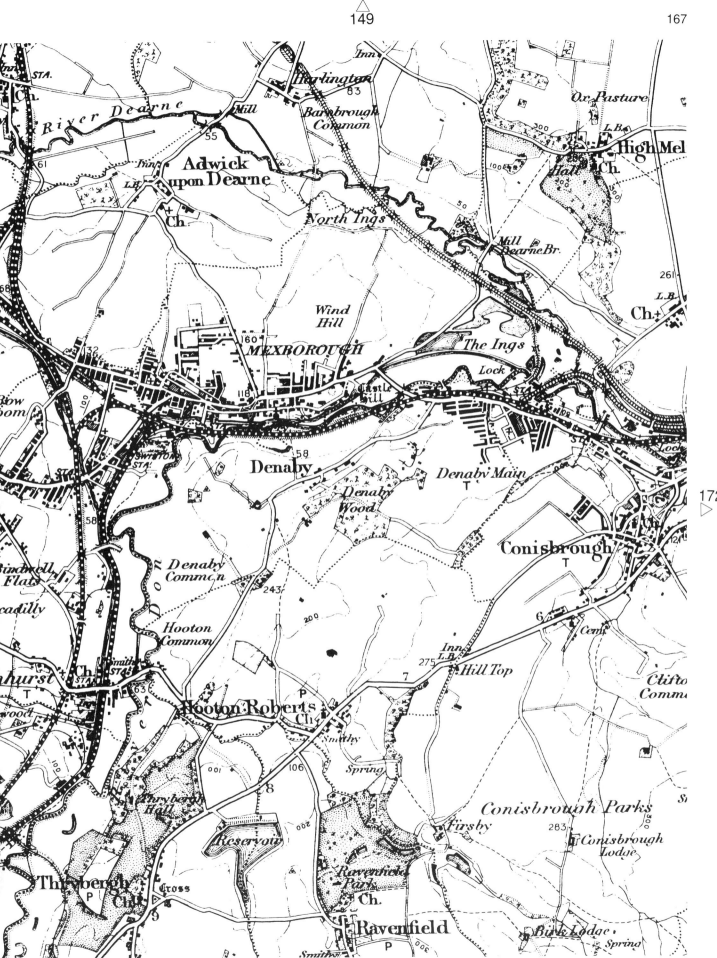

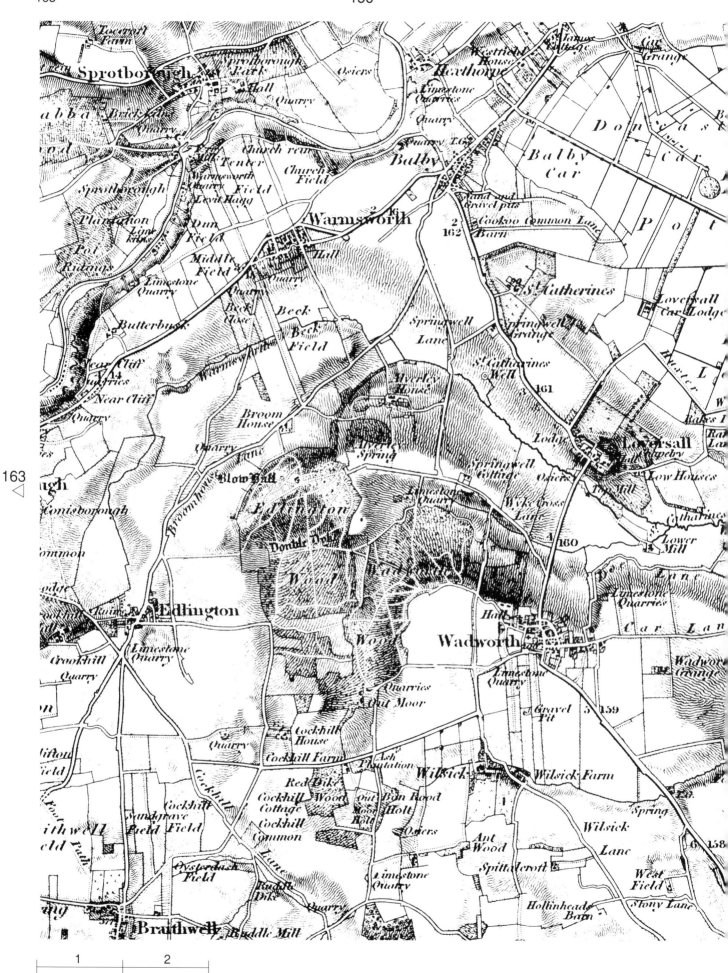

1 mile approx.

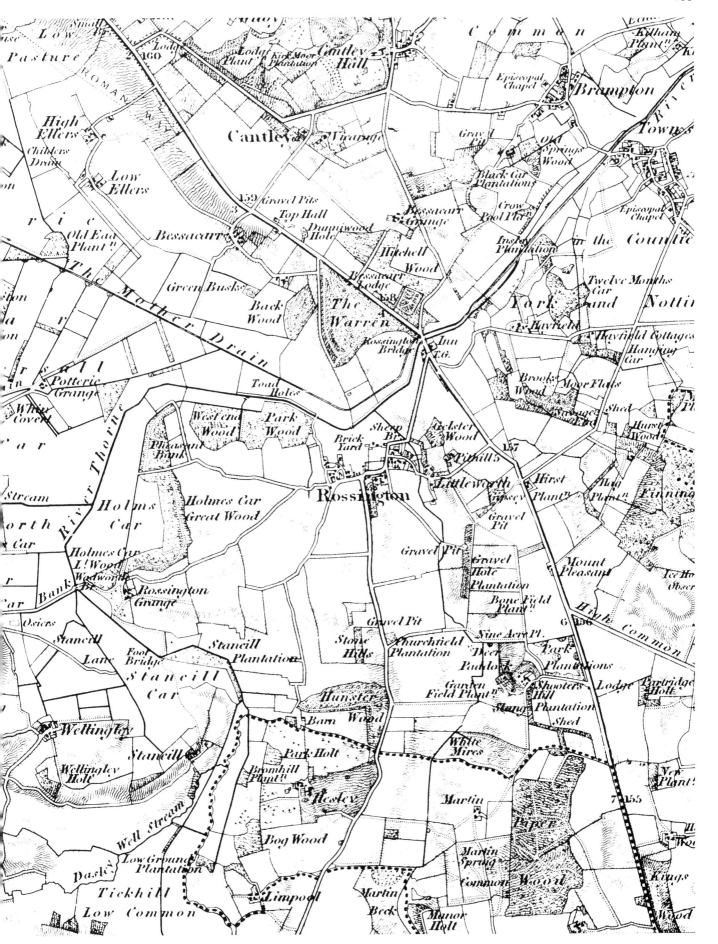

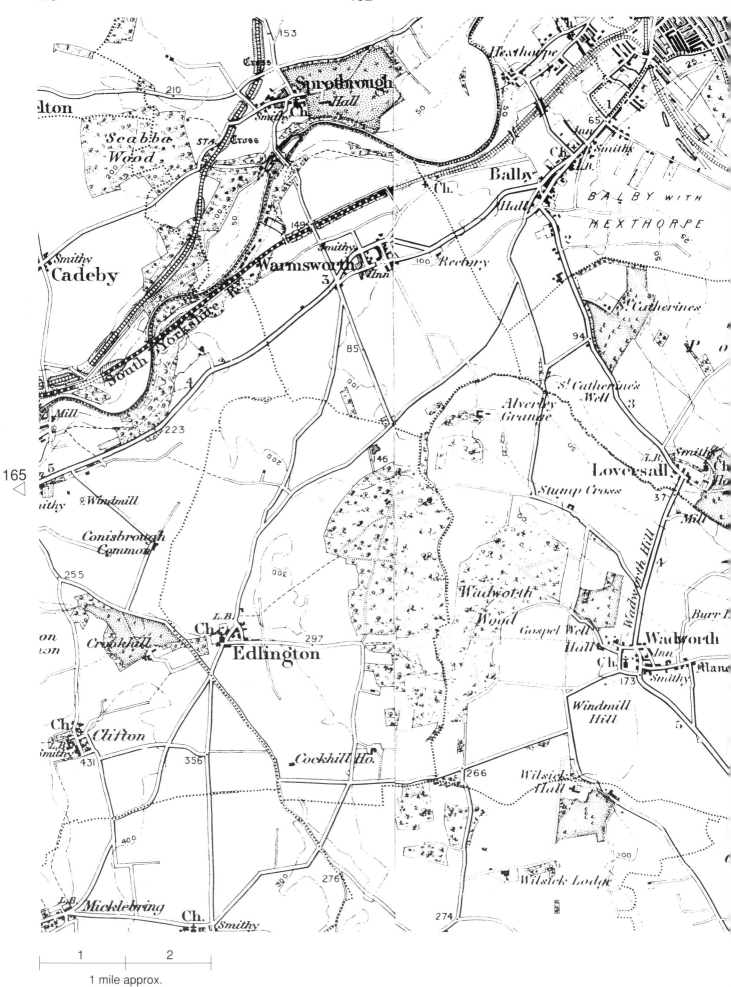

1 mile approx.

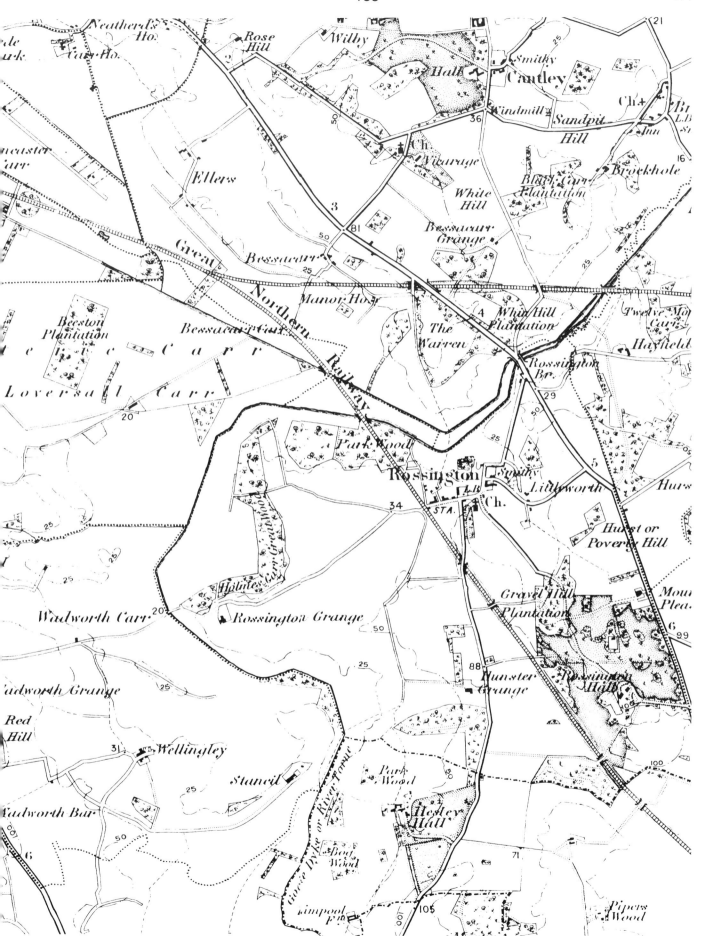

Surveyed 1871 - 72 / 1884 - 91. Revised 1894. Published 1895 - 96.

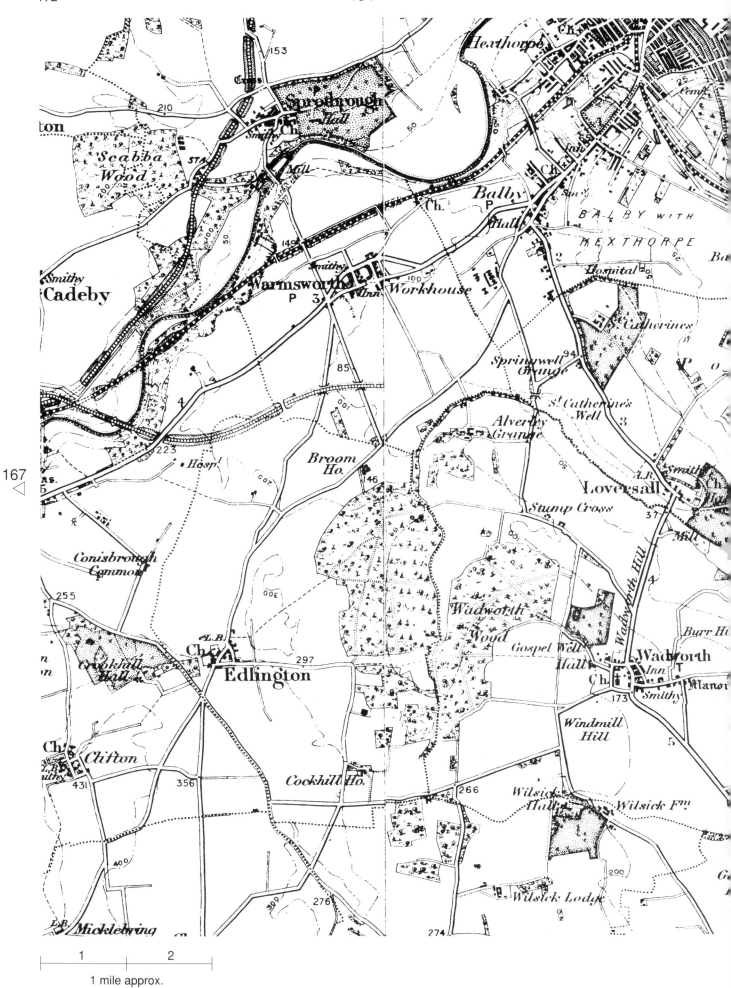

154

167

1   2

1 mile approx.

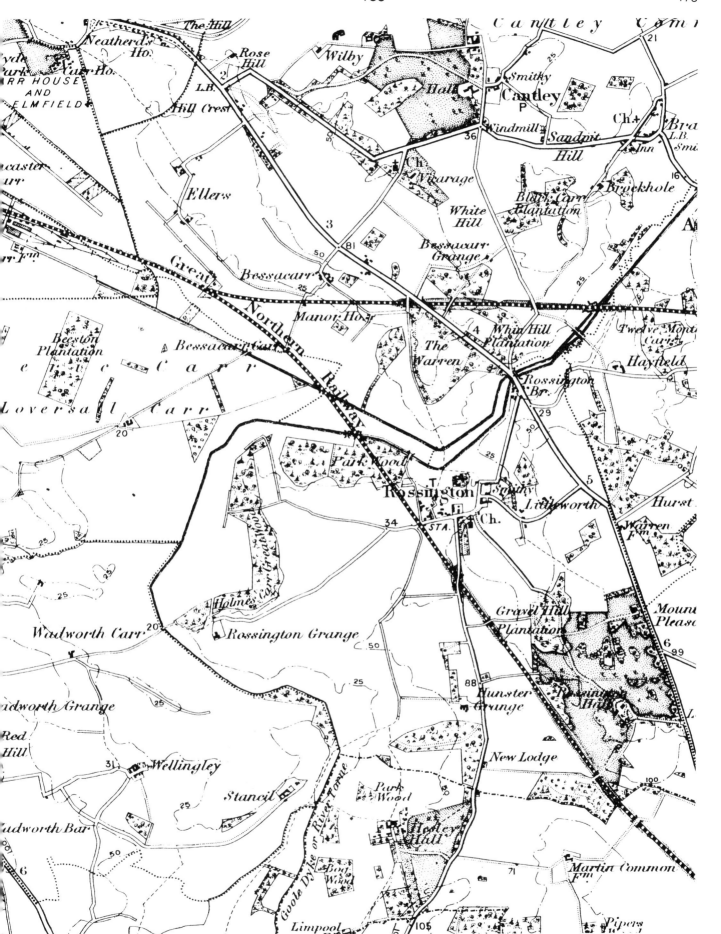

Surveyed 1884 - 91. Revised 1905. Published 1907.

1 mile approx.

Published 1840.

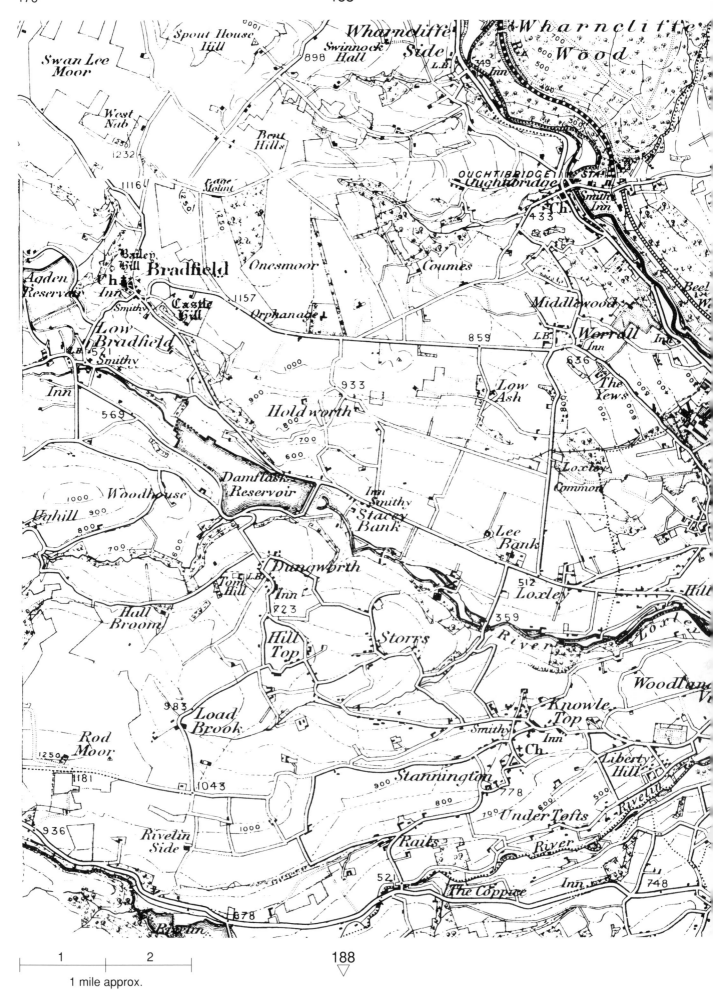

Swan Lee Moor

Spout House Hill

Swinnock Hall

Wharncliffe Side

Wharncliffe Wood

West Nab

1232

Bent Hills

OUCHTIBRIDGE STA.

Oughtibridge

Cave Mount

1116

1250

Ch

433

Bailey Hill

Bradfield

Onesmoor

Coumes

Beel

Agden Reservoir

Ch

Inn

Castle Hill

1157

Middlewood

Worrall

Inn

Low Bradfield

Smithy

Orphanage

859

Low Ash

636

The Yews

Smithy

569

933

Holdworth

900

800

Loxley Common

Woodhouse

1000

Damflask Reservoir

700

600

Inn Smithy

Stacey Bank

Lee Bank

Uphill

900

800

700

600

Dungworth

Loxley

512

Tom Hill

Hall Broom

Inn

823

Storrs

River

359

Hill Top

983

Load Brook

Knowle Top

Smithy

Inn

Ch

Liberty Hill

Rod Moor

1250

1181

1043

Stannington

778

900

800

Under Tofts

River

936

Rivelin Side

1000

Rails

River

748

52

The Coppice

Inn

678

Rivelin

1   2

1 mile approx.

Surveyed 1874 - 85. Revised 1894. Published 1896.

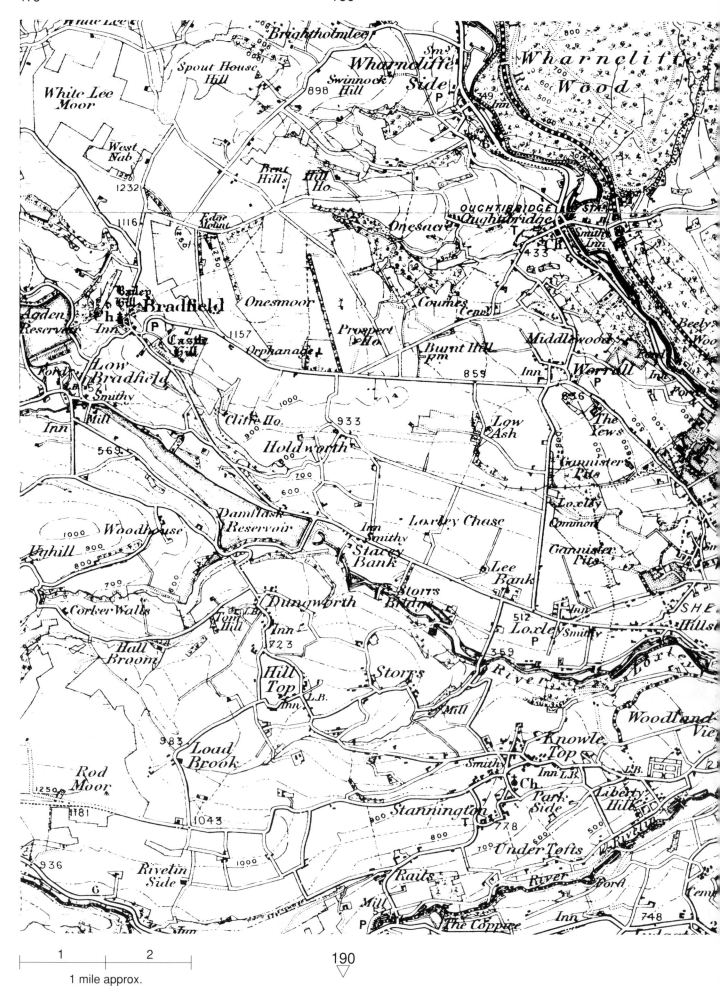

1

2

1 mile approx.

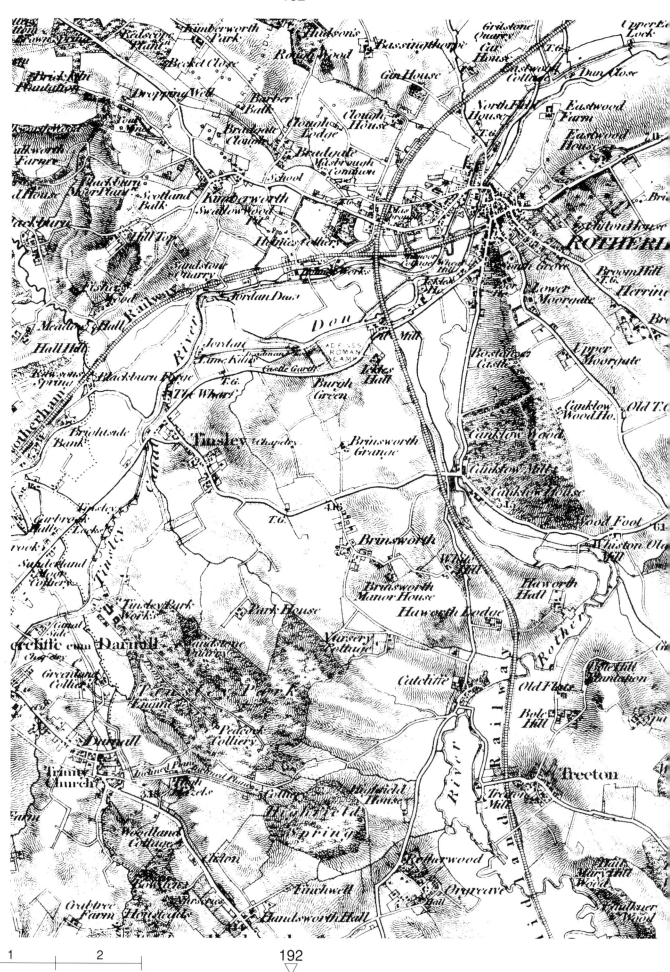

1   2

1 mile approx.

Published 1840.

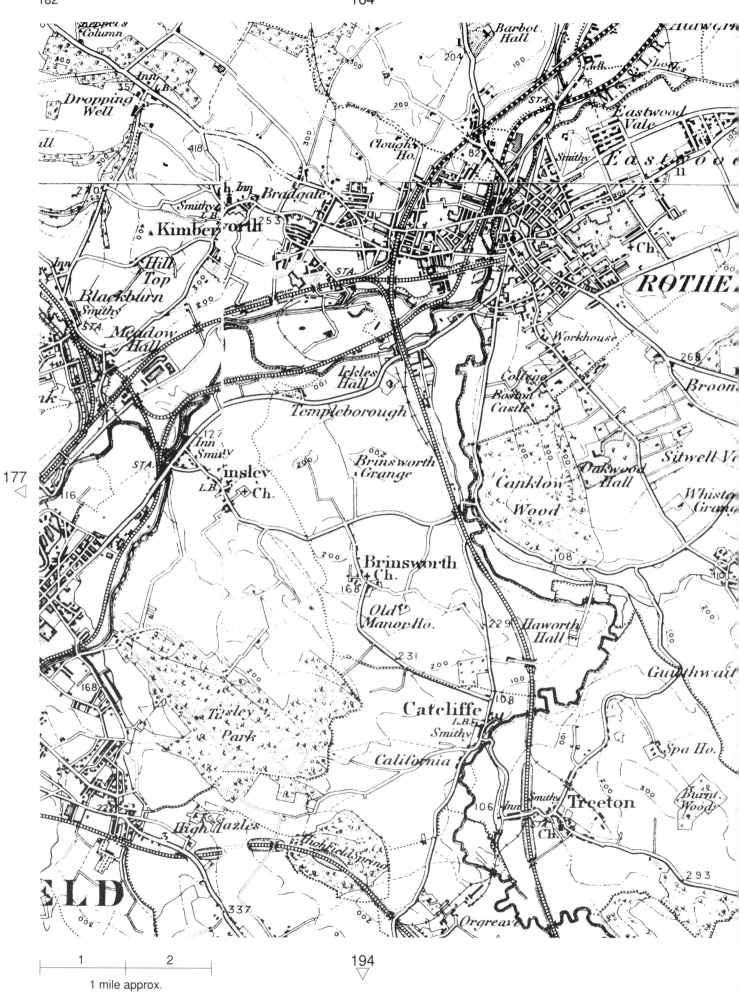

Keppel's
Column

Inn
L.B.

Dropping
Well

400

357

418

204

Barbot
Hall

100

STA.

76

Eastwood
Vale

Smithy

11

Clough
Ho.

300

200

82

h. Inn

Bradgate

Smithy
L.B.

Kimberworth

253

ROTHE

Inn

Hill
Top

300

Blackburn

Smithy

200

Meadow
Hall

STA.

STA.

STA.

Workhouse

268

Broom

College

Boston
Castle

Ickles
Hall

Templeborough

100

Oakwood
Hall

Sitwell V

127

Inn
Smithy

Brinsworth
Grange

Canklow
Wood

Whisto
Grang

insley

116

L.B.

Ch.

200

290

200

108

110

200

168

Brinsworth
Ch.

168

200

Old
Manor Ho.

229

Haworth
Hall

100

168

231

200

100

Guilthwai

168

Catcliffe

100

Tinsley
Park

L.B.

Smithy

Spa Ho.

California

200

300

Burnt
Wood

Treeton

106 Inn
Smithy

293

222

High Hazles

3

Ch.

LD

HighFieldSpring

337

200

Orgreave

1   2

1 mile approx.

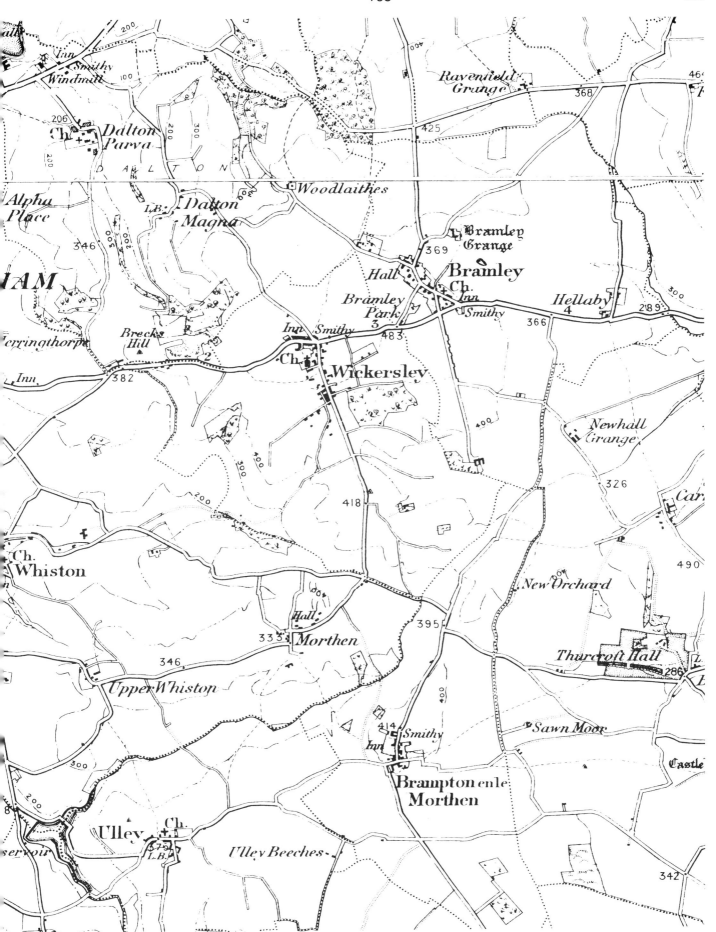

Surveyed 1874 - 85. Revised 1894. Published 1896.

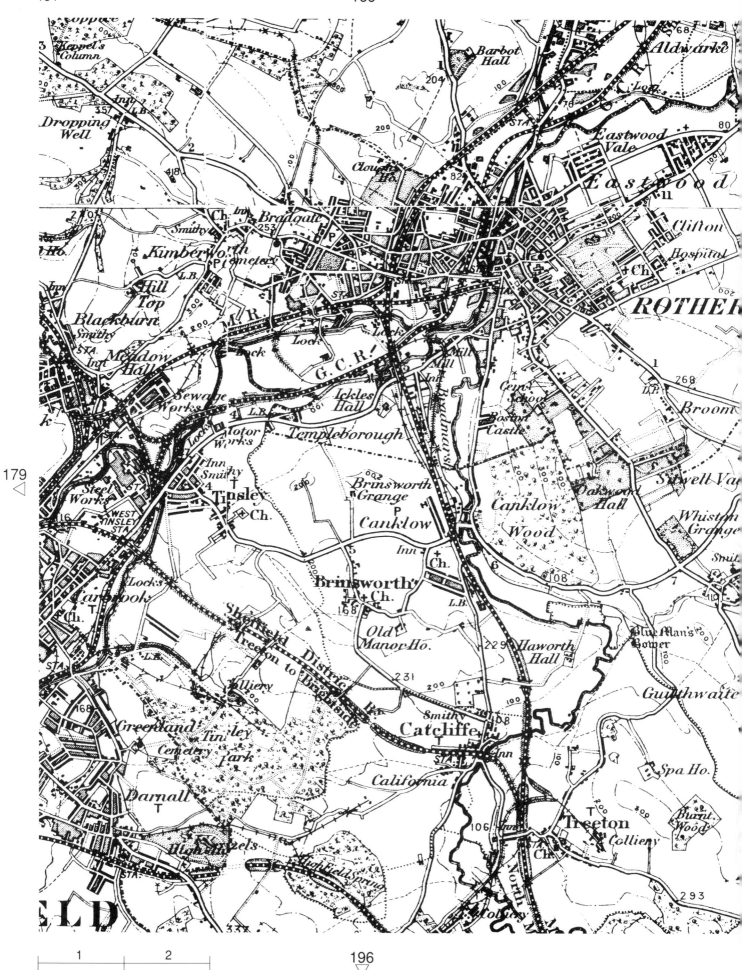

1   2

1 mile approx.

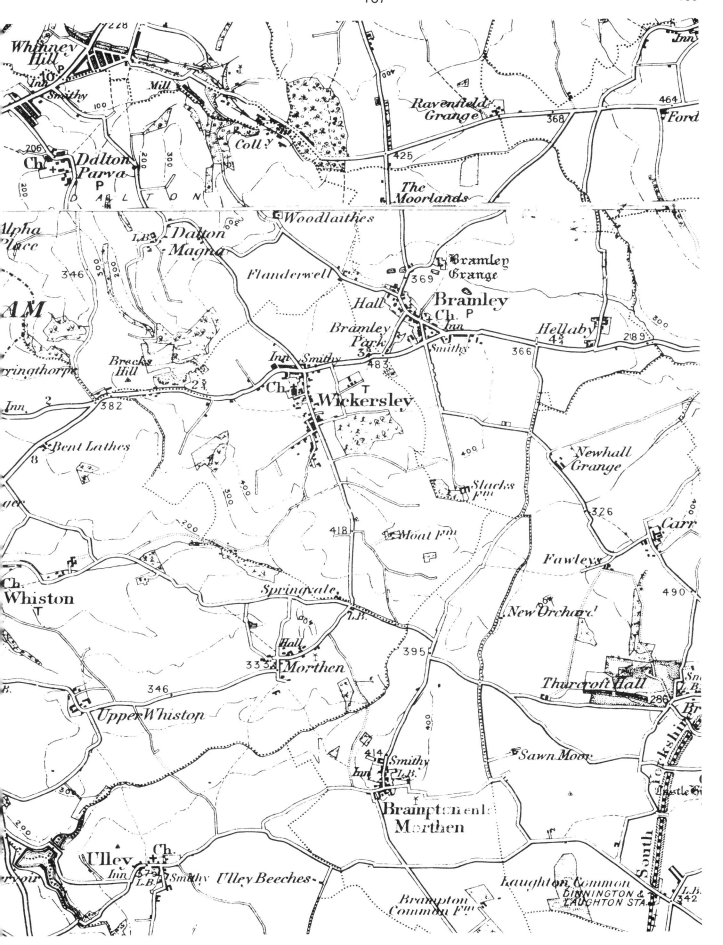

Surveyed 1874 - 85. Revised 1906 - 07. Published 1909.

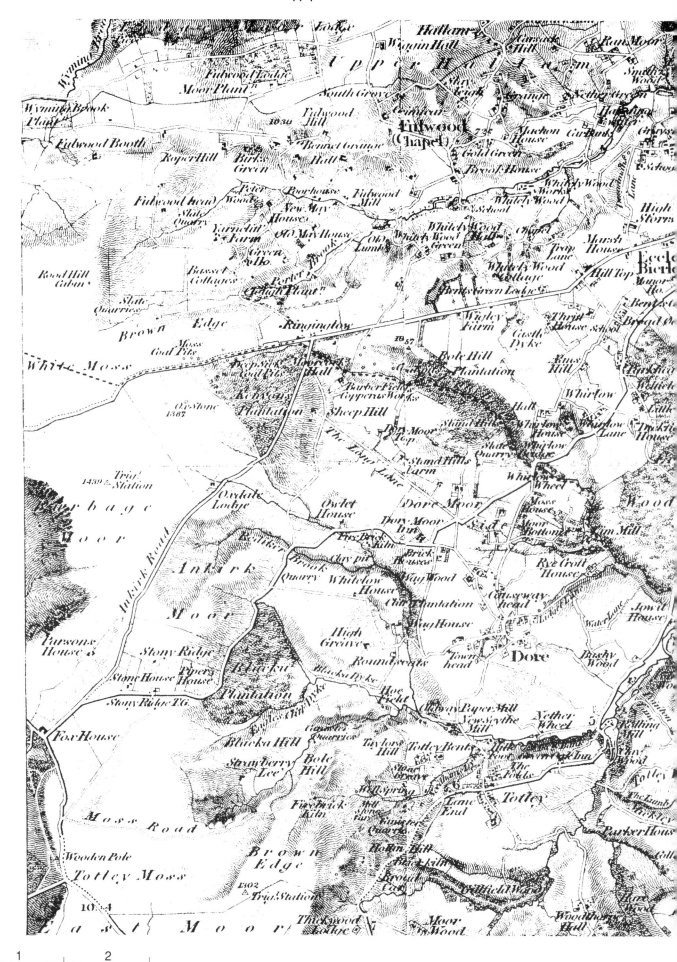

1   2

1 mile approx.

Published 1840.

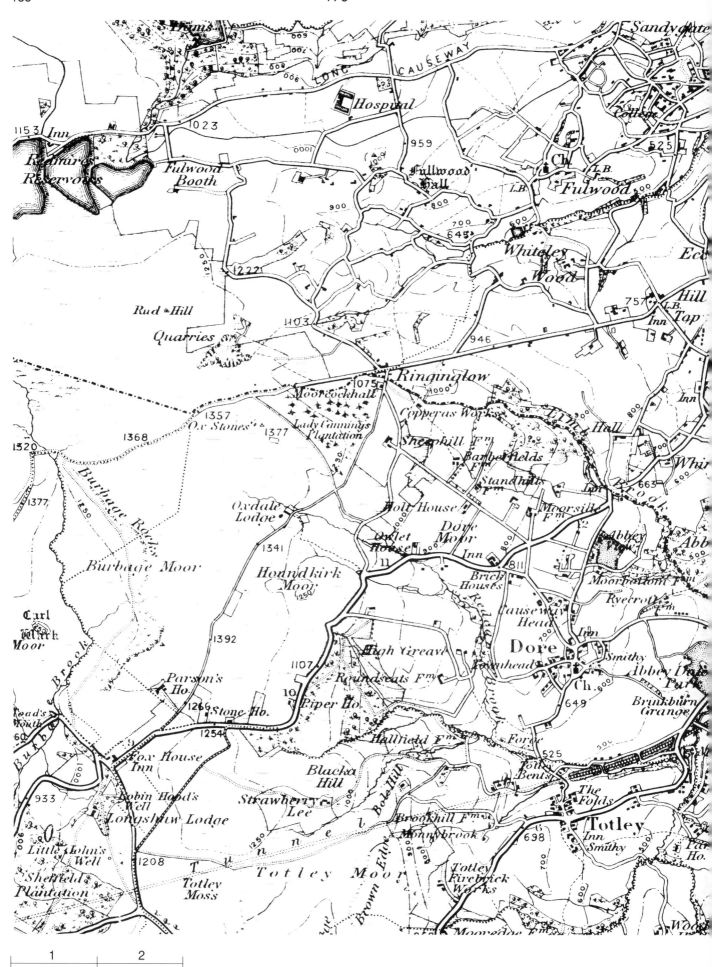

1 mile approx.

Surveyed 1874 - 85. Revised 1894. Published 1896.

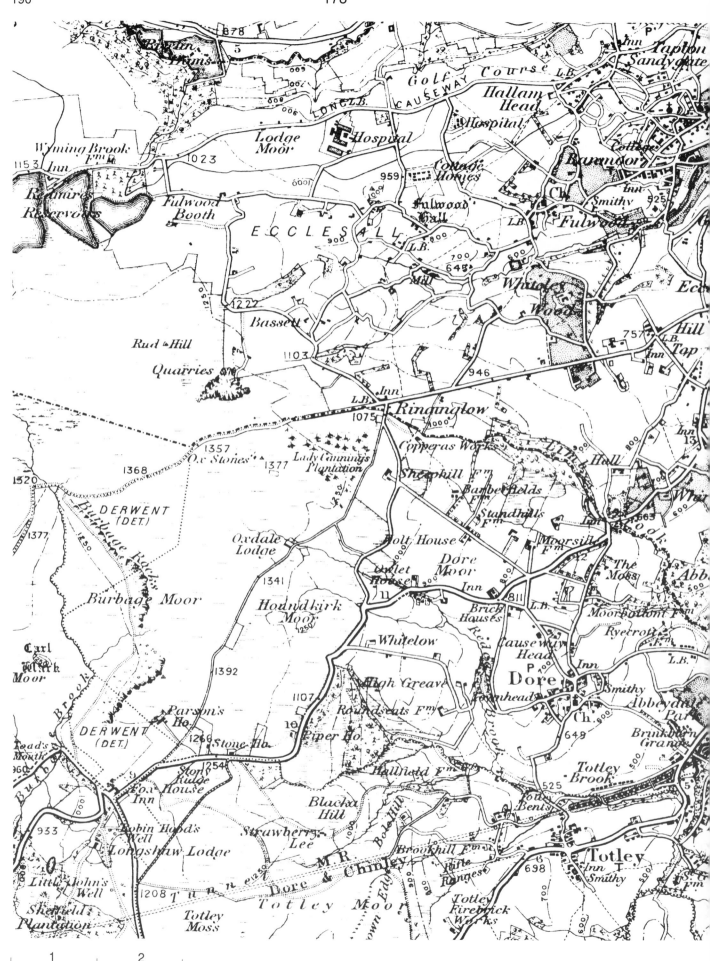

1 mile approx.

Surveyed 1874 - 85. Revised 1906 - 07. Published 1909.

180

Handsworth
Dore House
Faulkn...
Woodhouse Mills
Bramley Hall
Handsworth
Coalbrook Lodge
Grange
Fence Farm
Myrtle Bank
Ballfield Wood
Engine
Ballfield New Colliery
Richmond
Ballfield Hall
Shirtcliff Wood
The Bottoms
Richmond Hill
Woodthorpe Common
Woodhouse
Woodhouse Hill
Quarry
Yorkshire Bridge
Gill Dyke Wheel
Normanton Hill
Fountain Dam
Great Upper Wheel
Nether Wheel
Linley Bank Plantation
Linley Bank
Stratfield
Intake
Intake Colliery
Hollins End
Birley Vale Colliery
Mayfield Plantation
Inkersall Wheel
Rainbow Wheel
Hackenthorpe Wood
Treeton Crofts
Chapel of Ease
Ironstone pits
Birley Moor Farm
Quarry
Hackenthorpe
Drake House
Sothal
Engine
Coal pit
Birley
Birley Moor Colliery
Brook Lane
Drake House Lane
Nab Lane
Inkersall Wood
Orchard Lane
Base Green
Birley Hollins
Birley Moor
White Lane End
Birley
Sandstone Quarry
Birley Wood
Moor Hole Colliery
Hanging
Wood
Westfield Farm
Sand Holes
Phœnix Inn
Cam House
Moor Hole
Carter Hall Lane
Mosborough Moor
Mosborough Moor Colliery
Waterthorpe Farm
Phœnix Forge
High Lane
Cuckold Haven
Brick kiln
Coal pit
Knoll Hill Mill
Halfway House
Carter Hall
Carter Hall Wood
Ridgeway
Kent Wood
Newlands
Wren Park
Coal pit
Sandstone Quarry
Mosborough
Coal pit
School
Meeting House
Plumbley
Street Fields
Streetfield Colliery
Royds
Littfield
Cross
Plumbley Wood Lane
The Bushes
West Mosborough
Mosborough Hall
Oxcles Farm
Jeer Lane
Ford
Never Fear Wheel
Carlton Wheel
Lady Bank Wood
Dane Bank
Windmill Hill
Birleyhay
Old Sleeper
Summer Wood
Bridge Hill
Fields Wheel
Moss Brook
Rectory
Newlands Wood
Bramley Sough
Score House
High Bramley Wood
Back Lane
Park Bank
Castle
Tram Road
Great Fold Farm
Shady Hall
Warren House
Bramley Hall
Marsh Lane
Eckington
Southgate
Chapel Wheel
Cold Well
London Lane
Bramley Moor
Light Wood Farm
Setup Lane
Brick kiln
North Wood
Bramley Moor Plant
Bramley Moor Colliery
Lings Wood
Eckington Marsh
Tunnel
Renishaw

1   2
1 mile approx.

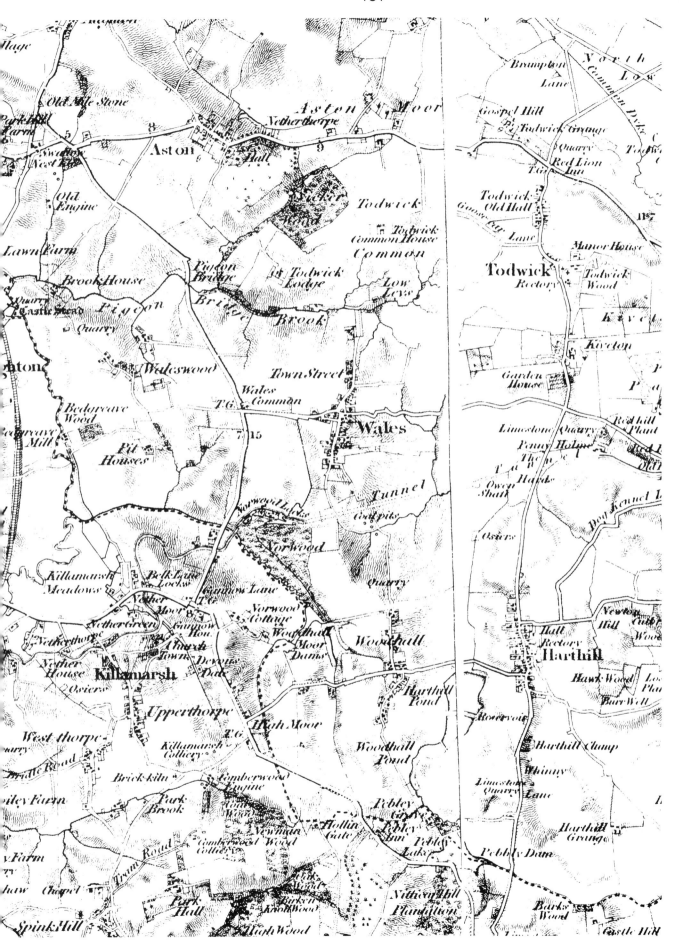

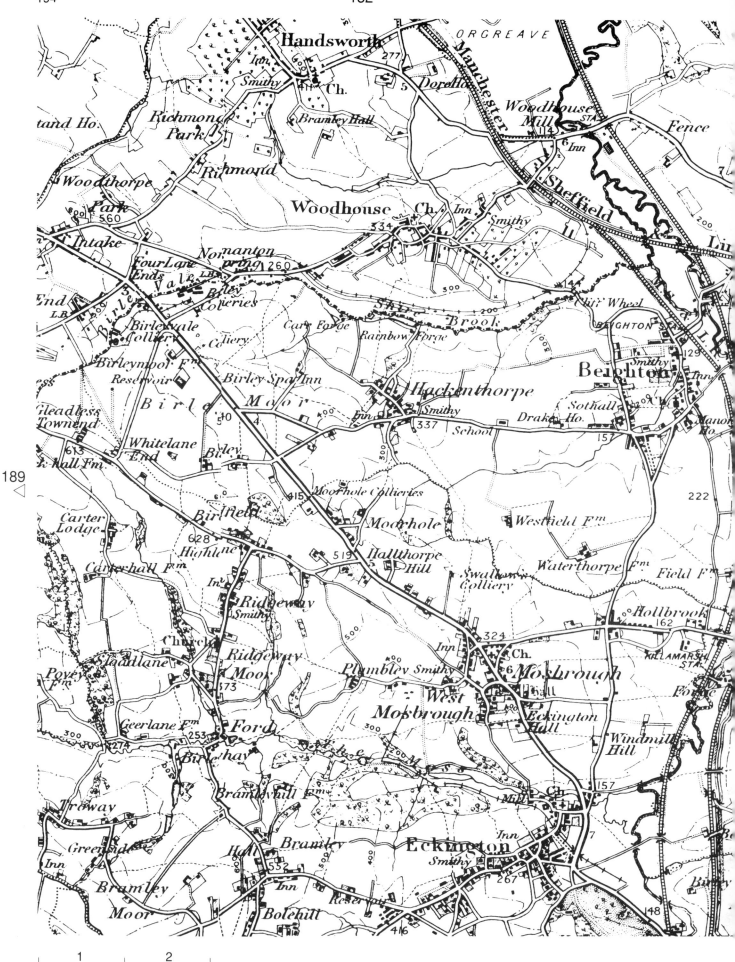

194

182

189

Handsworth

Inn
Smithy
Ch.
277
Dore Ho.
5
ORGREAVE
Manchester
Woodhouse Mill
STA
Inn
Fence
Bramley Hall
Sheffield
Richmond Park
Richmond
Woodhouse
Ch.
Inn
Smithy
Woodthorpe Park
560
334
Intake
Normanton Spring
260
Four Lane Ends
L.B.
Birley Collieries
Brook
Cinder Wheel
BEIGHTON STA
129
End
L.B.
Birleyvale Colliery
Colliery
Carr Forge
Rainbow Forge
300
200
Beighton
Smithy
Inn
Birleymoor F^m
Reservoir
Birley Spa Inn
Hackenthorpe
Smithy
Sothall
Drake Ho.
Manor Ho.
Gleadless Townend
613
Birle   Moor
510
4
Inn
337
School
15
Whitelane End
Birley
500
222
Hall Fm.
415
Moorhole Collieries
Moorhole
Westfield F^m
Carter Lodge
Birlfield
628
Highlane
519
Hallthorpe Hill
Swallownest Colliery
Waterthorpe F^m
Field F^m
Carterhall F^m
Inn
Ridgeway
Smithy
Hollbrook
162
Church
Ridgeway Moor
324
KILLAMARSH STA
Staddlane
573
Inn
Ch.
Mosbrough
Povey F^m
Plumbley Smithy
6
Geerlane F^m
Ford
300
West Mosbrough
Eckington Hall
Windmill Hill
274
253
Birchay
The
157
Troway
Bramleyhall F^m
Mill
Ch.
Greenside
Hall
Bramley
Eckington
Forge
Inn
552
Inn
Smithy
148
Bramley
Inn
267
Moor
Bolehill
416

1   2

1 mile approx.

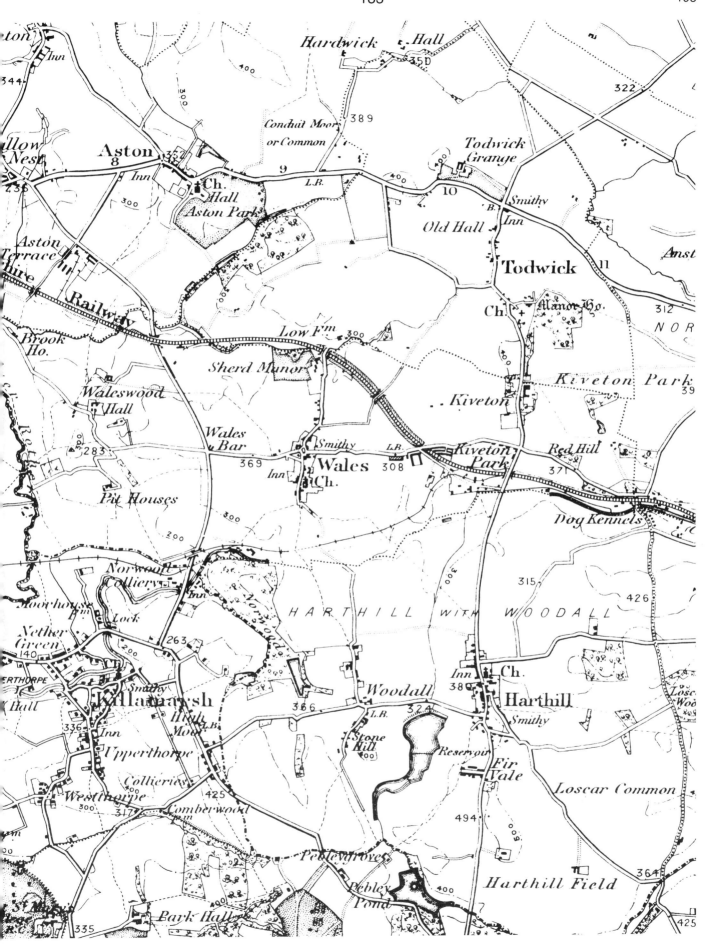

Surveyed 1874 - 85. Revised 1894. Published 1896.

△ 191

Orgreave

Handsworth
Cemetery
L.B.
Inn
Smithy
Ch.
277
Dog Ho.
ASTON
Woodhouse
Mill
114
Bramley Hall
Crabtree Fm
Richmond Park
L.B.
and Ho.
Woodthorpe Park
560
Richmond
WOODHOUSE STA.
Ch.
Inn
Smithy
Fence
Intake
Cem.
Four Lane Ends
Normanton Spring
Woodhouse
Cemetery
534
200
Viaduct
Inn
19
L.B.
Birley Collieries
260
L.B.
Inn
Shire Brook
300
BEIGHTON STA.
Car Forge
200
Birleymoor Fm
Reservoir
Birley Spa
Hackinthorpe
School Houses
P
Sothall
Drake Ho.
Beighton
129
Ch.
L.B.
Birley Moor
540
18
400
Ch.
337
Smithy
15
200
Manor Ho.
Headless Townend
615
Inn
Whitelane End
Birley
L.B.
500
222
Carter Lodge
Birchfield
415
Moorhole Collieries
Moorhole
Westfield Fm
628
Highlane
L.B.
519
17
Owlthorpe
Waterthorpe Fm
Field Fm
Carterhall Fm
Inn
P
Ridgeway
Smithy
L.B.
Swallow Colliery
Halfway Mill
Holbrook
162
373
Church
Ridgeway Moor
324
Inn
Ch.
16
Mosbrough
Inn
KILLAMARSH
Povey Fm
Stradlane
Plumbley
Smithy
West Mosbrough
Eckington Hall
Forge
Geerlane Fm
L.B.
Inn
Ford
253
300
Windmill Hill
Cemetery
274
Birleyhay
Bramleyhall Fm
157
Troway L.B.
ECKINGTON
CAMP
15
Greenside
Inn
Hall
Bramley
Inn
552
Birley
Bramley
Reservoir
Marshlane
148

1   2

1 mile approx.

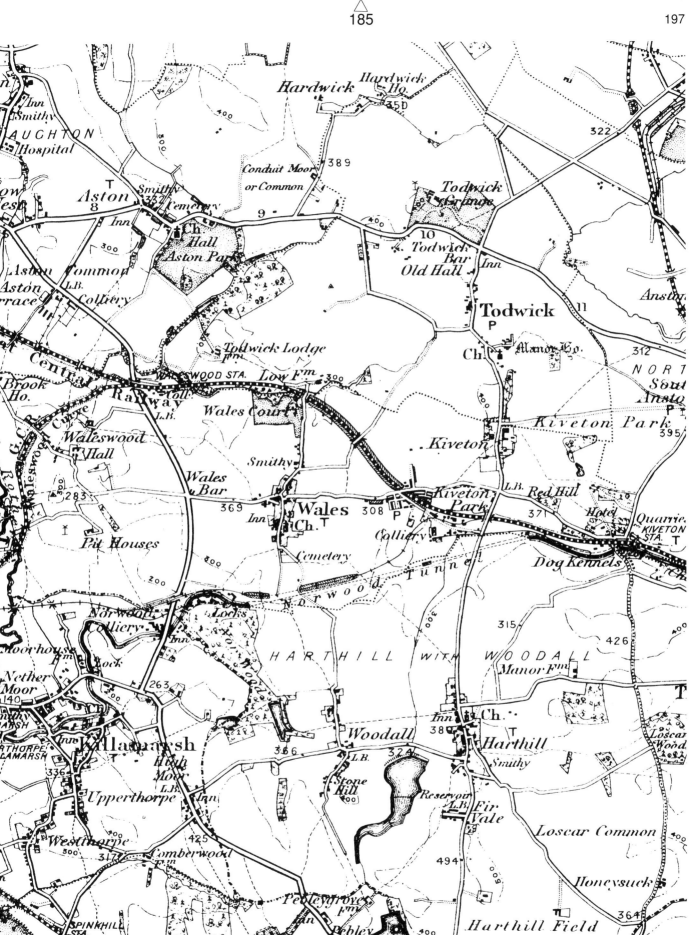

Surveyed 1874 - 85. Revised 1906 - 07. Published 1909.

Bibliography

The Victoria History of the Counties of England.
Editor: Christopher Elrington.
Publishers: Oxford University Press.

The Making of the English Landscape West Riding
of Yorkshire by Arthur Raistrick.
Publishers: Hodder & Stoughton. 1970.

Portrait of West Yorkshire by Margaret Slack.
Publishers: Robert Hale. 1984.

Gazetteer

The following list of place names is not definitive; rather it is designed to stimulate the reader's interest and, used in conjunction with a modern day atlas, assists on a journey of re-discovering one's heritage